The Making of Menander's Comedy

The Making of Menander's Comedy

by

SANDER M. GOLDBERG

University of California Press
Berkeley and Los Angeles

University of California Press
Berkeley and Los Angeles

ISBN 0-520-04250-6
Library of Congress Catalog Card Number 80-5322

Printed in Great Britain

Preface

The New Comedy may in certain respects be described as the Old tamed down, but in products of genius, tameness is not generally considered a merit.

> A. W. Schlegel, *Lectures on Dramatic Literature and Art* (1817)

It was Euripides who fought this death struggle of tragedy; the later art is known as the New Attic Comedy. In it the degenerate form of tragedy lived on as a monument of the most painful and violent death of tragedy proper.

> Friedrich Nietzsche, *The Birth of Tragedy* (1872)

In the [Greek] original, as always in such cases, everything was better ordered, collected, and to the point, and the model was accordingly more firmly joined, tight, and straightforward.

> Gunther Jachmann, *Plautinisches und Attisches* (1931)

Comparisons have not helped the reputation of Greek New Comedy. When seen as a pale shadow of past achievements or as a structural ideal which later Roman playwrights too often failed to duplicate, its own diversity, vitality, and theatrical power are easily forgotten. Yet New Comedy was the culmination of dramatic development at Athens, and it became a major influence on later western comedy. As long as its practitioners were only names and their plays fragmentary, comparison with such known quantities as Aristophanes and Euripides or Plautus and Terence was a necessary approach. The rediscovery of Menander in this century at last makes possible an examination of New Comedy – or at least Menandrean comedy – as a dramatic form in its own right. We shall indeed want to ask how the tradition developed and how it influenced later drama, but our main task is to see how Menander's plays worked on the stage as plays.

The following study is based upon the Greek text of Menander but quotes the plays in translation to open the discussion to a wider audience. Where a translation might seem to obscure a point or bias an argument, the Greek is also given. In translating Menander I have sought to be accurate without losing sight of the fact that he wrote dramatic verse that is highly effective and engaging. Published translations, none of which has proven entirely satisfactory, are cited in the bibliography. Menander's titles are perhaps the most difficult thing to translate gracefully; *The Rape of the Locks*, *The Unkindest Cut*, and *The Shorn Girl* all convey something of Menander's title *Perikeiromene*, but not its brevity. I have therefore decided to call the plays by their Greek titles and translate them only when necessary. Other Greek and Latin titles are translated or not as seemed appropriate. The principle guiding the choice will I hope seem more practical than erratic.

This work began as a doctoral dissertation written at the Institute of Classical Studies of the University of London in the academic year 1976–7 and submitted to the Department of Classical Studies at Indiana University. It is a pleasure to thank these institutions and the individuals whose co-operation and criticism have improved the work at every stage. The United States-United Kingdom Educational Commission made possible my year's study in London under the auspices of the Fulbright-Hays programme, and the staff of the Institute helped me settle into their superb library. Both Professor E. W. Handley and Professor W. G. Arnott read each chapter, made many helpful suggestions, and caught several errors. Those that doubtless remain are I hope due more to innocence than lack of energy. Special thanks go to Professor E. G. Turner for teaching the rudiments of papyrology to this willing, but not entirely adept pupil and for keeping me informed of the most recent developments in the textual field. On this side of the Atlantic, I owe thanks to Professor James W. Halporn, who as teacher, adviser, and colleague never let me forget that Menander wrote plays for the theatre, and Professor John Wright of Northwestern University, who first showed me what scholarship can do.

Stanford, California   S.M.G.
February 1979

Contents

I From Old Comedy to New   1

II Mapping the Terrain   13

III *Aspis* (*The Shield*): The Mixture of Modes   29

IV *Perikeiromene* (*The Shorn Girl*): Plot and Situation   44

V *Epitrepontes* (*The Arbitrants*): The Refashioned Recognition   59

VI *Dyskolos* (*The Grouch*): A Play of Combinations   72

VII *Samia* (*The Samian Woman*): A Play of Successful Combinations   92

VIII Menander and Life   109

Bibliography   122

Notes   125

Index   145

Abbreviations

Abbreviations of periodicals used follow the recommendations of the *American Journal of Archaeology* 74 (1970) 1–8. In addition the following abbreviations have been adopted for ease of reference:

Austin = C. Austin, *Comicorum Graecorum Fragmenta in papyris reperta* (Berlin 1973).

EH = *Fondation Hardt Entretiens XVI, Ménandre* (Geneva 1970).

G–S = A. W. Gomme and F. H. Sandbach, *Menander, A Commentary* (Oxford 1973).

K = T. Kock, *Comicorum Atticorum Fragmenta*, 3 vols. (Leipzig 1880/8).

K–T = Menander, *Reliquiae, pars altera*, 2 ed. by A. Körte and A. Thierfelder (Leipzig 1959).

Texts

This study is based upon the Oxford text of the Menander papyri edited by F. H. Sandbach and the fragments from literary sources as found in the Teubner edition of A. Körte and A. Thierfelder. Other Greek and Latin texts are cited in the editions of the Oxford Classical Text series with the exception of Aristophanes, who is cited from the Budé edition by V. Coulon and H. van Daele, 5 vols. (Paris 1923/30).

I

From Old Comedy to New

Mrs Warren: Well, keep yourself to yourself: *I* don't want you. But
             listen to this. Do you know what I would do with you if
             you were a baby again? aye, as sure as there's a heaven
             above us.
Vivie: Strangle me, perhaps.
Mrs Warren: No: I'd bring you up to be a real daughter to me, and
             not what you are now, with your pride and your pre-
             judices and the college education you stole from me
             . . .I'd bring you up in my own house.
Vivie: In one of your houses.
Mrs Warren: Listen to her! listen to how she spits on her mother's
             grey hairs! Oh, may you live to have your own daugh-
             ter tear and trample on you as you have trampled on
             me.

                                (Shaw, *Mrs Warren's Profession*)

Simo: What's the point? Why torture myself? Why wound
         myself?
         Why harrass my old age with this boy's foolishness?
         Should I pay the price of his misdeeds?
         No, let him keep her, go off with her, live with her.
Pamphilus: Father!
Simo: What 'father'? As if you needed this father!
         House, wife, children found without a father's blessing!
                    (Terence, *The Andrian Girl*)

From the social critique of Bernard Shaw to the romantic
comedy of Terence is not really a very great leap. The struggle
between Kitty Warren, whose unsavoury profession has made
her rich, and her daughter Vivie, whose respectable upbringing
those riches have financed, develops from questions of parentage and identity and the depiction of family conflict that we
can easily trace back through Sheridan and Shakespeare to the
ancient comedies of Terence and Plautus. Shaw claimed *Mrs*

Warren's Profession was a tract against the white slave trade, but his moral lesson works as a play because he translated it into personal terms by means of familiar dramatic mechanisms. The confrontation between Mrs Warren and Vivie is as inevitable and as crucial as that between Simo and Pamphilus. Each dramatist builds toward the moment. Each parent lapses into the third person in an effort to dismiss his child from his feelings, and each audience responds to the emotional charge of the scene. Shaw's modernity prevented the eventual reconciliation between parent and child that was a fixture of the tradition as Terence knew it. The sudden discovery that Pamphilus' mistress is indeed an eligible bride will reunite Simo and his son; we last see Kitty Warren as an unsuccessful mother who pays for her failure with the loss of her child. Yet the domestic building blocks of Shaw's play lie at hand in the comic tradition Terence exemplifies.

Though Terence exemplifies this tradition, neither he nor Plautus before him invented it. Comedies centering on family affairs developed first in Greece in the fourth century BC. It was there and then that separated lovers and angry parents began to dominate plays and where braggart soldiers and pompous cooks first established themselves as comic types. The flamboyant narratives of Falstaff and the culinary skill of Eliot's Alexander MacColgie Gibbs owe as much to the Greeks as to the Romans. Aristophanes' *Clouds* and *Wasps* exploit the comic potential of generations in conflict. Lamachos of *The Acharnians* boasts of his military prowess and Pisthetairos relishes the very thought of a meal in *The Birds*. But the fifth-century plays of Aristophanes subordinate these elements to a greater design. How did they grow to become the very substance of a comic tradition?

In 388 BC Aristophanes produced *Wealth*, the last of his surviving plays, which is significant in the history of drama because it looks back to the bold, fantastic comedy of the fifth century and also forward toward comedy of this very different sort. The plot centres on a poor but virtuous Athenian named Chremylos who arranges to cure the god Wealth of his proverbial blindness in the belief that a Wealth who can see will visit only the just. The cure is successful. Honest men become prosperous, and the play ends with a triumphant procession from Chremylos' house to restore Wealth to his rightful place on the Acropolis. Much of the action follows a familiar Aristophanic pattern. As in *The Acharnians*, where Dikaiopolis receives a wineskin full of peace, it hinges on the development of a fanciful conceit, and, like *The Acharnians* and *Birds*, it ends with a series of petitioners who hope to share in the hero's triumph. Even the Olympian gods are reduced to the status of petitioners since they no longer receive sacrifices, and Chremylos' central debate with a personified Poverty, who is indignant at her imminent expulsion from Attica, resembles the formal contest between opposing ideas known to scholars of Old Comedy as the *agon*. Yet beneath such familiar features lie sure signs of change. Some seem negative. The role of the chorus is much reduced, and the *parabasis*, in which the chorus steps out of its role to address the audience directly, is entirely lacking.[1] Elaborate choral songs have been replaced by notes in our manuscripts indicating the probable position of independent musical interludes. Word play is less common than in the past, and there is little of the sharp topical humour and spirited obscenity we think typical of Aristophanes. Other changes, however, have a positive side that indicates not simply the decline of old forms but the emergence of new ones.

Most apparent is the prominence of Chremylos' slave Karion. Dionysos, of course, had Xanthias to accompany him to the Underworld, and Xanthias was no colourless lackey. Yet he exists primarily as a foil to Dionysos and fades from view as the literary theme of *The Frogs* develops. Karion's role in *Wealth* is more consistent and of greater structural significance. In the expository dialogue that opens the play, Karion and Chremylos converse almost as equals. Karion also leads the chorus of old farmers, and his monologue describing Wealth's cure in the shrine of Asklepios is a dramatic highpoint. Finally, he joins equally with Chremylos in the task of receiving the petitioners to Wealth. Unlike Dionysos and Xanthias, who are larger than life and whose relationship is exploited with comic brilliance and a touch of the grotesque, Chremylos and Karion are drawn on a human scale and are, at least by comparison, realistic. The appearance of Poverty, Wealth, and Hermes to share the stage with them may recall the comic fantasies of the fifth century, but the more plausible representations of these human characters look ahead to later comedy. A second sign of change is the circumscribed scene. *The Acharnians* moved from the Athenian assembly place to Euripides' house in town to Dikaiopolis' country farm. In *Peace* Trygaios actually rode to heaven on a giant dung-beetle, and in *The Birds* two rogues built a city of bricks and mortar in the air. The action of *Wealth* takes place in the street outside Chremylos' house. By limiting himself to this colourless backdrop, which he expands only by narrative flashes describing action elsewhere, Aristophanes focuses attention on details of everyday life. The hired informer who seeks recompense from Wealth is a comic butt at least as old as *The Acharnians*, but the main thrust of Aristophanes' social criticism has turned from public to private matters: the adverse effects of virtue on Chremylos' finances, an old woman threatened with the loss of her gigolo, a priest helping himself to his god's sacrifices. These vignettes share the satiric tone of the character sketches Theophrastos was to draw half a century later. They are trenchant and incisive, but impersonal. Aristophanes has moved from writing topical fantasias to depicting what Thornton Wilder, in his preface to *Our Town*, was to call 'the generalized occasion'.

What do such changes mean for the making of plays? The lack of choral lyric brings the diction of comedy closer to everyday speech, and de-emphasis of the grotesque, whether in the form of choruses, humour, or spectacle, opens the way for increased representation of daily life and the foibles of recognizable character types. Comedy after Aristophanes increasingly reflected scenes and personalities to be found each day on the streets of Athens, and it developed a whole series of distinct figures such as cooks, soldiers, parasites, and hetairai (courtesans).[2] We find titles like *The Farmer, The Doctor, The Parasite, The Shoemaker*, as well as plays named after hetairai such as *Neottis, Thais*, and *Synoris*. Much of the humour in such plays was of a type still to be found on late night television and among stand-up comedians. A dramatist named Xenarchos, for example, thought the grasshopper fortunate because the female of the species has no voice (fr. 14K), and a fragment of Antiphanes preserves a classic one-liner:

He's married, in fact. :: What do you say? Actually
married? I just left him alive and walking
about!   (fr. 221K)

Other forms of humour are more sophisticated.

I'd always thought the Gorgons were
a bit of fiction, but a trip to the market
made me a believer. When I look at
the fish-sellers there, I immediately become stone.
I have to turn away when talking
to them, for if I see how they value
their fish, I'm frozen stiff.   (Antiphanes, fr. 166K)

Social comment is wry and not without a touch of resignation.

What is his race? :: The rich.
Everybody says this is the finest race.
No one ever sees poor aristocrats.
                              (Alexis, fr. 90K)

Whoever he was who invented that drinking song
that health is the finest thing picked it
right, but when he says that beauty is second
and wealth third, he was raving, you see.
After health should really come wealth.
A poor man's beauty is an ugly beast.
                         (Anaxandrides, fr. 17K)

Such comedies were rooted in the facts of daily life: eating,
sport, love, the marketplace, poverty and wealth. Their
strength lay in their human dimension, and they both enjoyed
and capitalized upon an immense following.

A text is really only one part of a play. There are also details
of actual production – staging, delivery, and the like – and, even
more important for our purposes, there is the effect the play
aimed to have on its audience. The Greek audience was always
a force with which to reckon. It was large and vocal, and it took
theatre seriously. Groups of travelling players brought drama
into the countryside, and written texts were in circulation
among those with the leisure to read them. At Athens itself the
revival of old tragedies and comedies was established on a
regular basis in the fourth century, and official texts of the
'classics' were maintained to curb the excesses of actors and

producers. The wooden structures of the great Theatre of Dionysos were rebuilt in stone with a stage widened to some sixty feet and an auditorium seating between fourteen and seventeen thousand people for the major festivals.[3] Xenophon says that the tragic actor Kallipides boasted of his ability to make this huge crowd weep, and Plutarch, writing some four centuries later, tells how the sight of a mother about to kill her son in Euripides' *Kresphontes* could bring them shouting to their feet in an effort to stop her. An ancient biography of Aeschylus claims that at the first sight of the Furies in the *Eumenides* children gasped and pregnant women miscarried. The fourth-century audience was no less demonstrative. One of Theophrastos' more repellent characters displays a boorishness not unknown in modern theatres: 'he claps when the rest have stopped, and hisses actors everyone else is enjoying; and when there is a silence he will lift his head and belch to make the audience turn around.' Plutarch tells how the fourth-century comic actor Parmenon prided himself on his imitation of a pig's squeal. Rivals finally resorted to bringing a real pig into the theatre, but when it squealed the audience only shouted, 'what's this compared to Parmenon's pig?' The pig was then released into the auditorium, and the resulting pandemonium created a new proverb.[4] The audience was also astute and critical. At the original performance of Euripides' *Orestes* in 408 a slip of the tongue by the leading actor Hegelochos made him a laughing stock for years. 'After the storm,' said Hegelochos, 'I see the clam ahead,' and neither the audience nor comic writers like Aristophanes ever let him forget the error.[5] Successful performances earned actors applause and eventually prizes in the fourth century, but a poor performance could easily bring catcalls and an angry stamping of feet. Demosthenes' enemy Aeschines, for example, began his career as an actor, and his more memorable failures gave his rival ample material for abuse. 'When he played the woes of Thyestes and the Trojan War,' Demosthenes reminded the Athenians, 'you drove him from the stage with hisses and all but stoned him to death' (*False Embassy* 449).

This continuous tradition of theatrical performance gave the Greek audience both experience and critical acumen, and a dramatist could enrich the effect of his play by drawing upon their collective memory. Consider, for example, this isolated fragment from the comic writer Antiphanes, who began producing plays in 385 BC:

> Tell me,
> what is life? I say it's drinking.
> You see how trees beside the wintry streams
> are moistened both by night and day
> and so grow great and fine,
> wmile those resisting, as if parched
> and thirsty, perish root and branch.   (fr. 231K)

The reverence for drink reflects a common motif of comedy in Antiphanes' time, and he gives it a comic touch by the solemnity and dubious relevance of his speaker's example. This incongruous solemnity has a specific source. The passage echoes a famous scene in Sophocles' *Antigone* in which Haimon pleads with his father Kreon to be flexible.

> You see how trees beside the wintry streams
> that yield preserve each twig intact,
> while those resisting perish root and branch.
> 			(*Antig.* 712–14)

Haimon's speech is the sort of thing educated Athenians recited at dinner parties, and Antiphanes was no doubt basing part of his effect upon the allusion. But how could the mass of his audience, which did not carry the classics of Attic tragedy in their heads, catch at least part of the joke? First, there is the vocabulary. 'Wintry streams' and, at least in Greek, 'root and branch' are high-sounding phrases typical of tragedy. Second is the metre.

Both tragedy and comedy are written entirely in verse, and a staple metre of the two is the iambic trimeter. Aristotle remarks in *The Poetics* that this is the metrical pattern most akin to ordinary speech, and like our own unrhymed iambic pentameter, it was the common metre for spoken dialogue and speeches. Greek verse patterns are determined by the quantities of the vowels and are often more distinct than our own, which depend on stress. The basic pattern of longs and shorts in the Greek trimeter is this:

$$\cup - \cup - \mid \cup - \cup - \mid \cup - \cup -$$

Tragedy affected a particularly rigid form. It regularly allowed a long vowel to stand in the first element of each of the three units or metra, but it was sparing in the substitution of two shorts for a long (resolution), and restricted its positioning of pauses and word ends in the verse. The most famous such restriction, now called after the eighteenth-century scholar Richard Porson who first noticed it, prevents a word from ending on the first element of the last metron if the vowel in that element is long. What all this means in practical terms is that tragic poets avoided those combinations and positionings of words that created conflicts between the dynamic pattern of the line as spoken and the quantitative metrical pattern.[6] Comic poets, however, admitted such conflicts freely. Resolution was permitted almost anywhere in the verse, and 'Porson's bridge' was not observed, thus creating lines more varied and collo-quial than the regular patterns of tragic speech. Tragedy and comedy had different styles of speaking, and the audience, which knew these styles by ear, could readily distinguish them. A comic poet seeking a special effect would sometimes adopt the metrical norms of tragedy. In a famous metrical joke at line 180 of Aristophanes' *Peace*, for example, Hermes, opening the door of Zeus' house to Trygaios, begins to speak in the tragic diction appropriate to a god. He is so taken aback by sight of the giant dung-beetle on which Trygaios has made the trip, how-ever, that he finishes the line with a prosaic exclamation that ignores Porson's bridge. As for our fragment of Antiphanes, the Sophoclean scansion of the borrowed lines is unmistakable, and the listener, even if unable to recognize their source, would undoubtedly say to himself, 'this sounds like tragedy.'

In addition to such metrical allusions and parodies, the comic dramatists of the fourth century could draw upon a vast array of dramatic devices, characters, and situations developed over the previous generations. Prologues to shape the audi-ence's understanding of events, messenger's speeches to announce offstage action, descriptions of feasts, sudden recognitions, *ex machina* endings were all established techniques offering possibilities to exploit and past histories to evoke as the dramatist chose. Yet none of the hundreds of comedies written after Aristophanes' *Wealth* was apparently of much interest after late antiquity. They ceased to be read, scribes ceased to copy them, and so they vanished. Alexis, Antiphanes, Diphilos, Philemon and scores of lesser writers are known to us only through brief passages and isolated words quoted by grammarians, antiquarians, and users of literary tags. The tradition itself lived on in the Latin plays of Plautus and Terence written two centuries later, and through them it has entered our own theatre. But the original Greek material vanished.

Until the present century the greatest of these losses was the plays of Menander, who was born at Athens in 342/1 and wrote plays until his death in about the year 292. He had only limited success in his own time, but later generations rated his poetic gift next to Homer's. Plutarch thought him far superior to Aristophanes, and the sophistication of his style and his talent for deft phrases made him extremely quotable. There are hundreds of short passages preserved in literary sources and an entire corpus of epigrams, many of dubious authenticity. We knew something of his considerable dramatic talent from such plays as Plautus' *Bacchis Girls* and Terence's *Brothers*, which were based upon originals by Menander, but until 1905 no extensive pieces of his own dramatic writings were known. In that year excavations at Aphroditopolis in Egypt brought to light a papyrus book of the fifth century AD that contained considerable portions of three plays and pieces of two more, and since then the picture has changed with remarkable rapidity. In 1958 scholars learned of the existence in a private collection at Geneva of a papyrus book that contained Menander's *Dyskolos* intact, and the 1960's brought still more plays to light in varying states of preservation. Discoveries are still being made. Menander thus comes to us directly from the ancient world without the intervention of medieval scribes and early printed editions and without the sometimes confusing annotations of ancient scholars. We are free to read and inter-

pret him in our own way, but this direct contact presents
special difficulties of its own.

The first lies in the physical condition of the texts. Papyrus is
a paper-like product made by compressing strips cut from the
stem of a reedy plant that grows abundantly in Egypt.[7] Though
warm dry desert sand preserves it well, it tends to split at the
ends with wear, and surface fibres can be stripped away. Our
Menander papyri were well used in their own day. The codex
found at Aphroditopolis was a discarded book used to seal the
mouth of a jar full of documents. A roll of *The Sikyonian* written
in the century of Menander's death was later cut to make a
papier-mâché mummy case, and only an elaborate process of
steaming and cutting separated the sheets and allowed them to
be read. We know the *Misoumenos* from fragments of different
copies of this very popular play found among the buried waste
of Oxyrhynchus. The papyri were often thus tattered when
they entered the ground, and centuries of burial have contri-
buted further damage. Our continuous texts of Menander must
in varying degrees all be products of painstaking decipherment
and restoration. This process has accomplished a great deal in
making Menander accessible to literary study, but there are
pitfalls for the unwary critic. Imagine that Edgar's words in Act
III of *King Lear* were preserved only on a single fragment with a
broken right edge and a dark stain in the centre. A papyrologist, who signifies gaps with square brackets and marks uncertain letters or the spaces for missing letters with dots, might
translate the lines – were they written in ancient style – like this:

CHILDROWLANDTOTHED KT[   ]ME

HISWORDW   TILLFIEFOHAND[

ISMELLTHEBLOODO [

Isolated spots of ink might allow him to restore 'dark' and 'was
still' with confidence, and his knowledge of traditional English
rhymes would probably suggest 'fum' to complete the second
line. But what then? Do we want 'come' to rhyme with 'fum', or
should it be 'came'? Was it a dark tower or a dark town? The

editor will not know for certain, and perhaps only later will someone connect this fragment with the poem by Robert Browning and so clinch the case for 'dark tower came'. And the last line? The logic that supplied 'fum' might well suggest the blood 'of an English man', and some editors might print that until, perhaps, the chance discovery of another scrap revealed that Shakespeare had actually written 'British' for 'English'.

A second kind of difficulty lies in the style of ancient books themselves, which were written by hired scribes without word divisions.[8] Our Egyptian manuscripts of Menander tend to be everyday rather than deluxe editions, and care is required to settle questions of articulation and set right the errors of omission and commission that result from rapid copying. To these problems, which are common to all hand-copied books, dramatic texts add special difficulties of their own. Entrances and exits are unmarked by punctuation, and stage directions of any sort are extremely rare. An initial list of *dramatis personae* was hardly universal, and though a character is usually identified in the margin the first time he speaks in a scene, subsequent changes of speaker are anonymous. The scribe simply put a line, called a *paragraphos*, in the left hand margin beneath the verse where the change took place. If the speaker changed within the verse he would add to the *paragraphos* either a small space at the point of change or two vertically arranged dots, called a *dicolon*. The *dicolon*, however, could also serve simply as a strong stop, a usage which sometimes makes a character's self-apostrophe in the middle of a monologue look like the comments of a second speaker. The system nevertheless works fairly well, but things can get muddled when the action is rapid. Suppose the murder of Banquo were printed like this:

SOALLMENDOFROMHENCETOTHEPALACEGATE
MAKEITTHEIRWALK:ALIGHTALIGHT:TISHE
STANDTOIT
ITWILLBERAINTONIGHT:LETITCOMEDOWN
OTREACHERY   (*Macbeth* III.3)

To add to the confusion, punctuation of this kind is particularly subject to loss or obliteration over time, and there is also evidence that ancient scribes copied these aides with less fidelity than they felt toward the text itself. Monologues pose problems of their own. Quotation marks and parentheses are non-existent, and even pauses are irregularly marked. A long messenger's speech in *The Sikyonian*, for example, which includes a narrative within a narrative and the direct quotation of speakers at a public assembly, appears in our papyrus without a bit of punctuation, and much scholarly effort has been required to interpret the speech correctly and punctuate it for the benefit of modern readers. It is small wonder that in Plutarch's day the learned orator Dio Chrysostom advised the student of Menander to have the plays acted out by professionals to avoid the preoccupations of private reading (18.6).

Modern editors of Menander must thus not only print the texts that these papyri have preserved, but they must visualize the action and supply those aides we so often take for granted in our printed editions. They have done the work well, but serious literary problems remain. The tradition of New Comedy proved to be remarkably fertile. It supplied the raw material for the Roman comedies in Greek dress known as *palliatae*, and the preservation of Plautus and Terence in medieval manuscripts brought the tradition into the modern world. Shakespeare's *Comedy of Errors* and Molière's *L'Avare* are direct adaptations of Plautine plays. Characters and scenes from the tradition found their way into the Italian *commedia dell' arte* and thus into the plays of Goldoni, while eighteenth-century English comedy adopted its interest in family relationships to give us the masterpieces of Sheridan and Goldsmith. Shaw and Wilde drew heavily on the comedy and pathos inherent in recognition plays, and there is more than a touch of Terentian delicacy in the characters of Wilder's *Our Town*. The seeds of renaissance comedy, of the comedy of manners and of character, and even of modern situation comedy are all to be found in the work of Menander, but they are not all so very apparent. Menander's plays, especially when read in translation, sometimes seem flat and predictable comedies of intrigue and misapprehension. The aim of this study is to bring them to life, to identify the techniques that make them work as plays and to demonstrate the vast potential of the ancient tradition that was to grow in so many different directions.

Mapping the Terrain

Menander's comedies, though major landmarks in the history of western drama, still remain something of a strange country with a shadowy history and an ill-charted topography. We have about a hundred titles, but the papyrus discoveries of this century have restored to us only one play complete (*Dyskolos*), substantial portions of five (*Aspis, Epitrepontes,Misoumenos, Perikeiromene, Samia*), intriguing excerpts of *Sikyonios*, and fragments of barely a dozen more. The major papyri range in date from the fragmentary roll of *Sikyonios* written in the century of Menander's death to the famous Cairo codex from Aphroditopolis, which dates from the fifth century of our own era. Because survival has been largely by chance, we do not know how representative of Menander's work our sample is. Nor, for that matter, do we know how well it represents the span of his activity. Only the *Dyskolos* has a probable date, which is 316. Menander produced his first play in 321, at about the age of twenty, and Plutarch says he was at the height of his powers when he died. Our knowledge of the comic tradition within which he worked is equally vague. We have seen how comedy continued to thrive after the production of Aristophanes' *Wealth*, but our odd fragments on papyrus and in literary sources do little to help us reconstruct the changing comic tradition. Yet the hallmarks of a strong tradition are apparent on every page of Menander. There is, for example, only a restricted set of characters appearing in similar roles with the same names and perhaps masks.[1] Smikrines will be an old, often miserly man. Moschion is a young lover, and Daos is a faithful slave. Sostratos, Gorgias, and Charisios are also young men, Demeas and Laches fathers, Getas and Parmenon slaves. The cast may also include minor characters drawn from a limited number of one-dimensional stock types, such as a cook or parasite, who introduce familiar jokes and recognizable patterns of speech. A second hallmark is the limited number of dramatic situations and settings. The extant plays all deal with either a young man's difficulty in getting a girl or with an estranged couple reunited. These are domestic dramas, and if not actually set in town are sure to take place near somebody's house. A third hallmark is structural. The plays all conform to a pattern of five acts separated by unrelated musical interludes. A chorus, often described as a band of tipsy revellers, is introduced at the end of the first act and thereafter appears at regular intervals without further mention. Such signs of convention stand as landmarks in the country but leave great spaces between them unmapped.

'Menander and Life,' runs a famous ancient epigram, 'which of you imitated which?' Menander's dramatic world of ravished maidens, simple young men, and angry fathers yet manages to present a formidable variety of dilemmas and faithful representations of human behaviour. Charisios' realization in the *Epitrepontes* that he has been punishing his wife for his own fault and Demeas' appeal to his son Moschion in the *Samia* not to let the wrongs of a day outweigh a lifetime's generosity are compelling dramatizations of human emotion. How does Menander make his conventional elements yield such convincing effects, and how, for that matter, does he make them into such a variety of different plays? Aristotle realized that one way to analyze the effect a piece of literature can have is to break it into its components and see how it is put together. *The Poetics* emphasizes at the outset that it is an analysis of the poetic craft and that the poet is a 'maker'.[2] A play is, after all, a deliberate construction built of elements chosen for their effect, and that series of choices determines both its structure and the impression it makes on an audience. To reach some understanding of Menander's comedy we shall have to examine how his plays are made, paying particular attention to the opportunities the tradition offered and the ways he chose to utilize them. To do so we must study the texts themselves, but we shall also want models to help us understand the dynamics of playmaking. Let us step back a little and consider first those models available to Menander himself and then those models our own distance from him thrusts upon us.

The *Synoris* of Diphilos contained a scene in which a woman, probably the hetaira of the title, and a parasite have the following exchange over the dice table:

S. You had good luck with your last throw.
P. You're sweet. Stake a drachma.   S. I did before.
I wish I could throw a Euripides.   P. Euripides
will never save a woman. Don't you know
from his tragedies how he hates them?
He likes parasites, though. That's why he says:
'He who has an ample living
but will not feed three men a day,
may he perish on his homeward way.'
S. What, in God's name, is that from? P. Never mind.
It's not the play but the thought that counts.   (fr. 73K)

The fragment suggests several things about fourth-century comedy. Hetaira and parasite are well documented comic types, and Diphilos was evidently willing to give them a certain prominence. Their contrived humour, initiated by Synoris' gratuitous wish for a 'Euripides', works on several levels. First is the pun, obvious to Diphilos' audience, on a 'Euripides', which was a throw of the dice, and the poet's name. There is also the superficial truism about Euripidean misogyny evident to anyone with a slight knowledge of his work. Third is the quotation itself, deliberately offered without context, which some might recognize as a compilation of a line from the *Antiope* (fr. 187 Nauck) and the *Iphigenia at Tauris* (535) joined by the parasite's own necessary addition. Of even greater significance is Diphilos' ability to assume a familiarity with Euripidean tragedy and to base the comic point of this exchange upon it. Diphilos was born sometime between 360 and 350; by the time he began producing plays Euripides had been dead some seventy-five years. Yet the fondness for him that Aristophanes satirized in his lifetime actually increased in the following century. The tragedies were often reproduced, written texts were in circulation, and passages from them were quoted both in real life and on the stage. Alexander the Great is said to have recited a scene from the *Andromeda* at his last banquet (Athenaeus 12.537d), and those infatuated with Euripides continued to be lampooned in comedy. Axionikos, who wrote in Antiphanes' day, produced a play called *The Euripides Lover*, and so did Philippides some years later. A character in Diphilos' *Parasite* (fr. 60K) calls Euripides 'goldplated' and, like the parasite of the *Synoris*, misquotes him for his own purposes. The continued life of the tragedies made possible an integral relationship between the comic effects of the fourth century and the most controversial tragedian of the fifth.[3]

Parody of the tragic is the most obvious manifestation of the relationship and is familiar from Aristophanes. Dikaiopolis' struggle to gain the good will of the Acharnians, for example, is made into a burlesque of Euripidean tragedy. He holds a sack of charcoal hostage to win a hearing from this chorus of charcoal burners, just as Euripides' Telephos apparently held the infant Orestes. When this fails, he makes a long speech that again parodies the *Telephos*. Between these two scenes is a more general play upon the diction, techniques, and mechanics of tragedy. Dikaiopolis decides to dress in rags to make his speech more pathetic and calls upon Euripides for help. A servant answers his call with the information that Euripides 'is inside and not inside', a bit of sophistry that parodies a favourite Euripidean mannerism (*Ach.* 396, cf. *Alc.* 521, *Hel.* 138). The poet is finally wheeled out of his house on the tragic *ekkyklema*. His language throughout the scene is comically grandiose, while the request for rags and Dikaiopolis' very desire to harangue the chorus reflect Euripides' fondness for tattered heroes and sophistic speeches. This episode illustrates several characteristics of comic parody. First, it derives much of its humour from its deliberate, gratuitous expansion. Dikaiopolis does not really need rags at all, but it takes him over twenty lines to coax the 'right' ones from Euripides. Second, it is blithely unfair. Dikaiopolis treats Euripides' plays as if they were a handful of stage properties, and Euripides complains that in demanding rags 'you are taking away my tragedies' (464, 470). And third, it is easily abandoned. Dikaiopolis' long speech to the chorus begins and ends with explicit parodies of the corresponding speech in the *Telephos*, but its echoes are spread over sixty lines. The speech is actually more political than literary and looks forward to the appearance of Lamachos, who will be Aristophanes' next target. After the intense literary parody of the preceding scene, the speech turns the comedy in another direction.

The effect of such parody comes from the incongruity of tragic diction and posture affected by a comic character for his own ends. We may compare the scene in the third act of Menander's *Aspis* where the slave Daos affects the posture of a tragic messenger from the house and announces a contrived calamity with a string of tragic quotations. But tragedy, especially Euripidean tragedy, offered the comic poets of the fourth century something beside material for incongruous allusions. As the most innovative dramatist of his time, Euripides demonstrated to his successors the wide range of effects Greek theatrical conventions made possible. Recent studies have emphasized his deliberate, sometimes daring experimentation and the increased, or at least altered potential for play-making his manipulation of the conventions made possible. A. P. Burnett, for example, lays particular stress on the extent to which Euripidean plays rely not only on the material they use, but on the audience's knowledge and expectations. 'The tragic plots were few,' she writes, 'even the fictions were few, and the poet, choosing among them, knew that each would evoke once more a unanimous trained emotion and a wealth of predictable association.'[4] Several Euripidean techniques, especially those which arouse and play upon expectations, found their way into comedy not as targets for fun but as integral parts of the dramatic structure. We shall need to distinguish between the parody of tragic devices for humour and the adaptations of tragic devices for a wider range of purposes.

Some adaptations result from common technical problems for which tragedy developed particularly fruitful solutions. Consider the preparation for an entrance.[5] The usual tragic practice was simply to announce the character's approach, and it made no difference whether the entrance was from *parodos* (i.e. from abroad) or from *skene* (i.e. from within). Thus, to cite two typical examples from Sophocles' *Oedipus*:

They signal me that Kreon is now approaching.   (78–9)

I see Iokasta coming from the palace.   (631–2)

The cue is visual whether the entrance is from Delphi or from the royal palace of Thebes. Euripides, for greater realism or perhaps simply to reduce the formality of such entrances, varied the formula by sometimes making sound the cue, either the sound of approaching footsteps (e.g. *Bacch.* 638–9, *Orest.* 1311–12) or the sound of the opening door (e.g. *Ion* 515. *Hel.* 858–60). In this way he was able to announce entrances more naturally, and by Menander's time we find the necessary announcements varied to suit the context. For example, to cite two from the *Samia*:

I see Parmenon coming from the market.   (280–1)

Apollo! The door is creaking again.   (567)

Although there is nothing intentionally 'tragic' about these entrance cues, their ancestry reveals the parallel craft of the two genres.

Another type of adaptation depends, like parody, upon a recognizable echo, but not intended to emphasize its incongruity. Such adaptations are blended into their surroundings as integral parts of the structure. The messenger's speech that opens the *Aspis* evokes the tragic without mockery; the title scene of arbitration in the *Epitrepontes* may owe something to a similar scene in Euripides' lost *Alope*, but not to parody it. Familiarity with tragedy made possible the reverberation of a motif, where the dramatist could build upon its tragic associations. The entrance of Euripides' Electra with a water jar, for example, had a certain shock value as the dramatist dethroned his heroine to reveal the magnitude of both her degradation and her pretensions. The Euripides of *The Frogs* was particularly proud of such domestic touches (*Ra.* 959ff.); a century later the memorable pose easily assumed tragic colouring. At *Dyskolos* 189 Knemon's daughter also enters with a water jar, and her opening exclamation of distress makes the tragic pose unmistakable. Her entrance introduces an element of the action that, as we shall see, is consistently represented by such recognizably tragic figures as this lamenting girl, a woeful messenger from within, and a stricken hero on the *ekkyklema*. The figures keep their tragic colour and, as elements integrated into the fabric of the play, affect the audience's perceptions of the action.

Our ability to recognize such echoes and to find prototypes for Menander's usage is aided by our knowledge of Euripides and Aristophanes, while the extant fragments of Menander's more immediate predecessors often help identify a comic *topos* or at least lead us to suspect one. Occasionally, however, such models are inadequate. When a more exact or dynamic model is required we are justified in looking to later comedy. The use of Plautus and Terence to illustrate discussions of New Comedy has long been an accepted practice, for the Latin texts, as deliberate re-workings of Greek plays, may be claimed to preserve the relevant aspects of their originals. Yet sometimes a more recent text, whose claim to our attention is not historical, may also help illustrate a point of technique. Some demands of play-making and some dramatic effects have remained remarkably constant through the centuries, and in such cases the practices of later dramatists may illuminate those of the earlier one.

Consider again that Euripidean 'quotation' in the *Synoris*.

ἀνὴρ γὰρ ὅστις εὖ βίον κεκτημένος
μὴ τοὐλάχιστον τρεῖς ἀσυμβόλους τρέφει,
ὄλοιτο, νόστου μή ποτ' εἰς πάτραν τυχών.

Had the parasite not announced that he would quote Euripides, the observance of Porson's bridge and the absence of resolved long syllables in these lines would still make them stand out from their context. Even the bogus second line conforms to the strict practice of tragic trimeters and contrasts with its surroundings, for resolution is otherwise common in this fragment and no two successive lines observe the bridge. In other cases, where context does not make the quotation so obvious, the cue must be different. At *Frogs* 1471 Aristophanes expects his audience to recognize Dionysos' 'my tongue swore' as an allusion to a notorious Euripidean line (*Hipp.* 612, cf. *Ra.* 102, *Thesm.* 275–6). At *Aspis* 432 perhaps only Daos' manner indicates that this single line is a quotation; at 415 we do not know if he is quoting tragedy or not.[6] How ought we to imagine the effect of such incorporated quotations on an audience? Here an example from our own drama illuminates the effect by analogy. The central character of John O'Keeffe's *Wild Oats* is

an itinerant player named Rover who delights in fitting life to
the language of his art. In the second act he flirts with Jane, the
maid of Lady Amaranth, in the presence of Jane's brother, Sim.

> Jane: Perhaps the gentleman might wish to send her lady a com-
>   pliment. An't please you, sir, if it's a kiss between us two, it
>   shall go safe; for, though you should give it me, brother Sim
>   then can take it to my lady.
> Rover: 'I kiss'd thee e'er I kill'd thee.'
> Jane: Kill me!
> Rover: 'No way but this, killing myself to die upon a kiss!'
>   (kisses her, Sim forces him from her)
> Sim: Go!
> Rover: 'Ay; to a nunnery, go, go.'

Many will recognize the tag from *Hamlet* and probably the lines
from *Othello* as well. The effect, however, does not depend upon
precise identification, though the incongruous allusion to
Othello's final passion may heighten the comedy for some. Nor
may an audience notice that those two lines are iambic. Rover's
manner alone can insure the comic point, even for spectators
ignorant of Shakespeare.

Parallel techniques of composition illustrate a further aspect
of the universal demands of play-making. Consider the distribution of roles. The opposed marriage, a common situation
in romantic comedy, requires three elements: a lover, a
beloved, an obstructor. The dramatist, however, must distinguish between these roles themselves – a structuralist would
call them 'functions' – and the actual characters he will have em-
body them.[7] The simplest way to dramatize the situation is to
assign each role to a different character, as Menander does in the
Dyskolos. This yields the familiar configuration of young lovers
and an obstructive old man. But that disposition is not fixed, as
another eighteenth-century comedy will remind us. The
opposition young Captain Absolute encounters in *The Rivals* is
not from his father but from Lydia Languish's romantic
attachment to poverty. He therefore courts her as the half-pay
Ensign Beverly while his father and Lydia's aunt press the suit
of Captain Absolute. The beloved is her own obstructor and the
lover his own rival, and we laugh at the inept but well-
intentioned efforts of the older generation to bring them

together. Sheridan has varied the stock situation by redistribut-
ing the roles. A similar redistribution shapes Menander's
Samia. Both young and old again desire the union, but Moschion has devised a scheme to avoid confessing that he has made
his intended bride pregnant. Each act ends with an obstacle to
the marriage removed, but each succeeding act introduces a
further obstacle generated by Moschion's initial scheme. The
young man unwittingly becomes his own obstructor as father
and son work at cross-purposes for the same end. By altering
the distribution of roles in the familiar situation Menander
creates different plays in the *Samia* and *Dyskolos*, and comparison with *The Rivals* illustrates how universal a part of the
dramatist's art this power of distribution is.

A related aspect of composition is point of view. What information will the dramatist give the audience, and what will he
hold back? What action does he dramatize, and what action
does he only report? With which characters will he have the
audience identify, and which ones will he hold at a distance? In
the last act of *The Winter's Tale*, for example, two actions take
place, the recognition of Leontes' lost daughter Perdita and the
return of his wife, Hermione. By only narrating the former
while staging the latter Shakespeare subordinates one action to
the other, thereby giving a distinct shape and emphasis to what
might otherwise be a disparate string of romantic motifs.
Menander's ability to make new plays from a limited store of
elements owes much to a similar ability to offer and hold back
characters and information, controlling the audience's perspective on events and thus making each dramatization different. In the *Epitrepontes* he represents the marital crisis of
Charisios and Pamphile largely through surrogates; in the
Perikeiromene and *Misoumenos* the principals enact their own
drama of estrangement and reconciliation. Knemon is the central character of the *Dyskolos*, though the plot concerns Sostratos' love for his daughter, because each step in the action is
developed as an approach to him. The ability to draw upon the
audience's experience and expectations, to vary the allocation
of roles, and to alter the perspective from which events are seen
give the dramatist considerable scope for making distinctive
plays from a limited range of elements. How Menander made

use of these possibilities will become clear through analysis of his work, but it may prove helpful to specify at the outset three general sources of creative variation constantly at work.

The first is what I shall call the mixture of modes. By a mode I mean the complex of devices and diction with their attendant connotations that in the drama of Menander's time was characteristic of either tragedy or comedy and thus either serious or light.[8] The hetaira and parasite of Diphilos' *Synoris* remind us that stock characters were an established part of Menander's tradition, and they frequently represent a light mode. The dramatic value of these stock types lies not in their humanity but in their deliberate flatness. A favourite such character in Menander is the cook, whose self-important loquacity was a fixture of the comic stage. The cook of the *Samia*, for example, first enters to relieve the tension of a dramatic monologue, and Menander uses him throughout the third act as a comic pacing device. The main event of the act is Demeas' expulsion from his house of his mistress Chrysis, and Demeas' harsh and unjust act makes for a serious and potentially ugly scene. The plot will require Demeas' neighbour Nikeratos to take Chrysis in, but Nikeratos, who has been developed as a comic foil to Demeas, is too absurd a figure to be swept into a serious scene without affecting its tone. Menander therefore delays Nikeratos' arrival until the necessary moment, but he reserves a place for him by having the cook present from the beginning. His presence for the confrontation is made natural by having the other characters come onstage to find him already there, and his unsuccessful effort to intervene introduces the comic note and role later assumed by Nikeratos. Because the cook has no individual identity the comedy he introduces remains a minor factor in the action until picked up and expanded by the more significant figure of Nikeratos. Use of the cook to introduce the light mode enables Menander to integrate a serious scene into his play without compromising the consistency of his action or characters.

Representatives of the serious mode are often products of that adaptation and integration of tragic devices previously discussed. The *Sikyonios*, for example, contains a long messenger's speech incorporating significant echoes of tragedy. The conversation introducing it is marked by tragic diction,

and though our text is fragmentary, the link with a famous
messenger's speech in Euripides' *Orestes* is unmistakable.

> ἐτύγχανον μὲν οὔ[
> βαίνων, μὰ τὸν Δί', οὔτε τ[
>]ε τοῦτ' ἐμοί

I happened to be coming not . . . , by heaven, nor . . .
> (*Sik.* 176–8)

> ἐτύγχανον μὲν ἀγρόθεν πυλῶν ἔσω
> βαίνων, πυθέσθαι δεόμενος τά τ' ἀμφὶ σοῦ
> τά τ' ἀμφ' Ὀρέστου.

I happened to be coming from the country to
the city gates wanting to hear news of you and
of Orestes.   (*Or.* 866–8)

We know from a number in the margin of the papyrus that this
speech began at about line 725 of the complete text, and so it,
like the corresponding speech in the *Orestes*, comes late in the
play, and it too describes an assembly debating the fate of an
important character. Menander's speech apparently maintained the function of its prototype, and echoes of Euripidean
language keep the audience aware of the tragic parallel.
Menander's purpose, however, does not seem to be parody.
Unlike Dikaiopolis' address to the chorus at *Acharnians* 496 ff.,
which also echoes a Euripidean speech, there is no sign of
incongruity in the messenger's tragic diction, nor does he seem
to affect his posture.[9] Instead, the suggestion of tragedy here
works, like the recognition scene of the *Perikeiromene* with its
tragic vocabulary and metre and like the opening of the *Aspis*
with its own solemn messenger, as a signal to the audience that
these events have a serious side. The tragic device keeps its own
colour and value in the dramatic structure.

Some of Menander's finest effects come from the juxtaposition of the two modes. At the beginning of the *Aspis* Daos speaks
with tragic solemnity of a military catastrophe abroad while
Smikrines, who interrupts him with questions, is revealed to be
the miserly old man of comedy. For Chrysis' expulsion in the
Samia and Pataikos' discovery of his children in the *Perikeiromene*
the presence of a cook or, as it happens, Pataikos' son Moschion

speaking in comic trimeters controls the emotional temperature of a powerful dramatic scene. The modes are the product of Menander's tradition, but his use of them constitutes one of the most fruitful bases of his originality.

A second source of creative variation necessitates a distinction between the plot of a comedy and the situations from which that plot is built. The reduced function of the chorus and the actors' loss of padding and phallus are external manifestations of a movement away from fantasy that is among the most striking changes in comedy between Aristophanes and Menander. The plays present action of human dimensions based upon the consistent and the reasonable. A wineskin full of peace and a kingdom among the birds are not the goals of Menandrean characters. The situations in which they find themselves may sometimes have small claim to probability, but their responses to those situations are pre-eminently human. Menander de-emphasizes such necessary improbabilities as a clandestine pregnancy or an unsuspected relative living next door by relegating them to the status of expository givens while he makes the dramatised action appear natural and therefore credible. Whereas Aristophanic comedy, to paraphrase Cedric Whitman, based its effect on the evasion of boundaries and the creation of an independent reality, Menander's plays draw heavily on a more normal range of experience, and each action generates the next with a logic that approximates our own.[10] Truly narrative plots are a major component of his comedies, and he takes care to make them coherent and well motivated. They also show considerabe variety despite the fact that the material from which they are made has distinct limits. The source of this variety becomes clear once we distinguish between a plot and a dramatic situation.

By 'situation' I mean what George Bernard Shaw, in his preface to *How He Lied to Her Husband*, called a 'stage framework', the position of characters at a given moment. We may liken it to the arrangement of pieces in a chess problem represented by the initial diagram. The *Misoumenos*, for example, includes three; an estranged couple, a reunion of parent and child, a betrothal. These and similar situations, all furnished by the tradition, are the components of the plot. 'Plot' is thus the succession of situations that makes the individual play. If the situation, to continue our analogy, is the arrangement of chessmen at a given moment, plot is the sequence of moves that constitutes the actual game. The relatively small number of situations in Menander's tradition yields plots of recognizable types, but the situations can generate other sources of individuality. As Terence observed of Menander's *Andrian Girl* and *Perinthian Girl*,

> qui utramvis recte norit ambas noverit:
> non ita dissimili sunt argumento, set tamen
> dissimili oratione sunt factae ac stilo.

> Whoever knows one well knows them both.
> They are not very different in plot, but they
> *are* made with different thought and expression. (*And.* 10–12)

The two plays evidently had the same story line (*argumentum*), but differed in their representation of events (*oratio*) and in their tone (*stilus*). Similarly, the *Perikeiromene* employs the same three situations as the *Misoumenos*, but by forging other links between them Menander makes a rather different play. The distinction between plot and situation will enable us to specify such similarities without obscuring the uniqueness of each play. It will also highlight the relationships among constituent parts of a single play's action. The double plot, either nascent or developed, found in such Terentian plays as *The Andrian Girl* and *The Brothers* remains without parallel in extant Menander. We find instead situations, such as Demeas' disrupted relationship with Chrysis and Moschion's reunion with his father and sister in the *Perikeiromene*, that enrich the action of the play without being developed in their own right. Disparate situations serve only to move the main action to its close, and it will prove helpful to speak of multiple situations but only a single plot in each play.

The alteration of elements familiar from the tradition provides the dramatist with a third source of variety. Euripides dressed the hero of his *Telephos* and *Helen* in rags; Menander's *Perikeiromene* and *Misoumenos* present comic soldiers who have lost their bluster. An entire scene may be refashioned for a new effect. The gatekeeper scene of both comedy and tragedy, for example, generally displays the hero's resolve and sets him on the way to his goal. At *Libation Bearers* 653ff. Orestes makes a considerable racket before the gates of Aigisthos' palace and receives a curt, but respectful reply. He immediately commands the porter to announce him and quickly passes on to the main confrontation as the anonymous porter is replaced by Klytaimestra herself. The usual comic variant is to delay the hero at the door by protracted conversation with an abusive or incredulous gatekeeper. Both Strepsiades and Dionysos experience such delays (*Nu* 131ff., *Ra.* 35ff.). Aristophanes stretches the familiar pattern at *Birds* 53ff., for there is no door at all, only a rock, and the gatekeeper is a bird. By basing their confrontation upon the familiar pattern Aristophanes can play upon the expectations aroused by Euelpides' 'knock' and by the appearance of a man-sized hoopoe. Nevertheless, Euelpides and Pisthetairos, like Dionysos, Strepsiades, and Orestes, manage to reach their goal. Euripides, however, can thwart the progress of the scene and confound all expectations by combining the tragic and the comic variants. The gatekeeper of the *Helen* is incredulous *and* abusive (*Hel.* 435ff.). Like Orestes, Menelaos seeks entry to a palace, but his attempt to command is interrupted in mid-sentence. The old woman answers his call with an abrupt command to leave, and he very nearly does just that. He breaks into tears, and his only resolution is to hide and creep away if the situation becomes too dangerous. By allowing the abusive porter of comedy to get the better of his ostensible hero, Euripides achieves a startling reversal of the tragic norm, and our shock at Menelaos' defeat becomes crucial to our perceptions both of him and of the play itself.

Gatekeeper scenes are rare in extant Menander. Pyrrhias narrates one at *Dyskolos* 97ff., but Sostratos later retreats from a door rather than confront Knemon. Sostratos is a weak character, and Menander avoids putting him in a scene characteristic of a strong one. The fragmentary fourth act of the *Aspis*, however, does preserve the remains of a gatekeeper scene as Kleostratos returns from captivity and seeks entry to his uncle's house. He bangs resolutely and exuberantly on the door, and Daos at first replies with a porter's cool terseness. But the familiar pattern has several twists. Kleostratos' enthusiasm wilts at the news, which is soon revealed to be false, that his uncle is dead, and the scene changes to a recognition scene between Kleostratos and Daos just as the papyrus breaks off. It also comes quite late in the action, for Kleostratos plays an *ex machina* role. Menander uses the gatekeeper scene to prepare for the climax rather than to initiate the action. Whereas Euripides altered the characterization in his scene while maintaining its familiar position and function, Menander has preserved its role but changed its position. It is the beginning of the *Aspis* that alters an expected characterization to produce a surprising effect. The baggage train accompanying Demeas and Nikeratos in the *Samia* and the procession of sacrificers in the *Dyskolos* are common forms of spectacle in comedy; little imagination is required to perceive the potential for bright and amusing action they represent. The procession that opens the *Aspis* is just the reverse. These people walk a death march and are followed by the mourning Daos carrying the battered shield of the title. The commotion of their entry brings Smikrines from his house, but the scene belongs to Daos.[11] His language and manner are entirely tragic, and his tale is one of pillage and death. Only a delayed prologue by the goddess Fortune is a clear sign that the action to come will indeed be comic.

This kind of shock, whether created by a cowardly king of Sparta or a comic slave cast as tragic herald, forces space between the audience and the figures upon the stage. The frustration of our expectations reminds us that we *had* expectations, that we are watching a play of a particular type, and the surprise of seeing familiar characters in unexpected roles awakens an interest that is more dispassionate and consciously amused. Daos' surprising and arresting appearance begins to build distance, and when Fortune then tells us that the source of his lamentation is an error, the extra knowledge puts the action further from us. We may come to share the intrigue against Smikrines, but at the same time we realize that the intriguers themselves are deceived. Greek theatre had no word for 'dramatic illusion', and we shall find it more helpful to think in terms of distance between audience and actors than of actors maintaining or breaking an illusion. Thus Smikrines and Daos open the *Aspis* with, to use one definition of dramatic illusion, 'the uninterrupted concentration of the fictitious personages of the play on their fictitious situation', but the surprise of their tragic scene fosters distance.[12] Moschion opens the *Samia* with a direct address to the audience, but his apparent frankness brings him closer to us and consequently narrows the gap. Menander's deliberate increase or de-emphasis of such distance is an important technique for giving individuality to his plays, and it comes as a direct result of offering and holding back information and his freedom in refashioning familiar devices to manipulate his audience's expectations.

The awareness of differing modes, the distinction between plot and situation, and a sensitivity to the creative use of traditional devices are the tools we shall use to map the world of Menander's comedy, for they are the same tools used in the making of it. Each of the following three chapters will concentrate on a single one of these tools, applying it to the examination of the structure of an individual, fragmentary play. We shall then examine how they worked together for the making of two plays we possess largely complete. The concluding chapter will turn again to constituent parts, examining the legacy bestowed on a wide range of successors and seeking to explain why Menander's plays, though in many ways such a strange country, sometimes seem so familiar.

Aspis (The Shield):
The Mixture of Modes

When a dramatist's characters and situations belong to a strong tradition and the course of his play is therefore largely predictable, he is apt to seek other sources of diversity. Variation in tone is a frequent recourse. As Carlo Goldoni observed of his own plays, 'I was certain that mine, which did not wander much from the ordinary and beaten track, would afford pleasure and even surprise from the mixture of comic and pathetic scenes I had artfully introduced.'[1] In the last act of *I due gemelli veneziani* Goldoni blithely poisoned one twin in order to bring his play to a joyous conclusion for the other. *Il servitore di due padroni* opens with the solemn betrothal of Clarice to a second suitor after her first, a certain Federigo Rasponi of Turin, has been killed in a duel. Complications develop when Federigo's sister comes to Venice disguised as her late brother, and the happy ending depends upon laying the dead man to rest once and for all. Goldoni clearly found death a convenient device for removing superannuated characters or motivating dramatic action, but the resulting contrast in tone also serves, like shadows in a romantic landscape, to emphasize the sunlight and make each play, though constructed of familiar elements, unique.

We find a similar use of contrasts in Menander, for whom the combination of serious and light takes two main forms. Tragic parody is the more obvious of these and is a trait Menander shares with all Attic comedy. It was common in Aristophanes, and by the fourth century the artificiality of tragic diction and the improbability of tragic situations had made the genre a favourite comic butt. The parody could be broad or subtle, consist of whole situations, whole lines of quotation, or only isolated words or allusions. We have already seen how

Dikaiopolis affects the posture of Euripides' Telephos when facing the angry Acharnians and how the parasite of Diphilos' *Synoris* invents a tragic quotation to serve his own ends. Familiar tragic tags could be used in different ways by comic poets. Euripides' *Auge*, for example, contained the lines, 'What nature wished is no concern of laws: for this was woman born.' Anaxandrides (fr. 67K) turned this into 'what the city wished is no concern of laws.' At *Epitrepontes* 1123–4 Menander's slave Onesimos quotes the Euripidean lines verbatim as he teasingly breaks the news to old Smikrines that his daughter has given birth unexpectedly. Such parodies share the same end: humour through cleverness and incongruity. Whatever element of tragedy the parodist touches immediately turns to comedy.[2] A second form of mixture is more complex and requires the concept of 'mode' developed in the previous chapter. This is the use of recognizably serious and light elements juxtaposed for the effect achieved by blending them. Each element, whether originally tragic or comic, is allowed to keep its own value, and the resulting combination creates a new dramatic effect. Precedent for such deliberate blending lies not in Old Comedy but in Euripidean tragedy, and use of it becomes a key device of Menander's dramatic technique. Both forms of mixture appear in the *Aspis*.

Much is made of assumed and pretended death in the *Aspis*. The dramatic situation – just the reverse of Goldoni's *Servitore* – is initiated by the false report of Kleostratos' death and resolved when the young man himself appears alive and well. The play opened with an announcement of death in battle. In Act II Daos seizes upon Chairestratos' more or less sincere wish for death to devise a scheme to foil the miserly Smikrines, who as oldest surviving male relative is entitled by Attic law to seek marriage with Kleostratos' sister, now heiress of his estate.[3] Chairestratos will pretend to die, thus diverting Smikrines' attention from Kleostratos' sister to his own daughter, whose inheritance will be larger. The scheme requires elaborate and solemn play-acting. As Daos says, 'We shall have to stage a tragic, unpleasant misfortune' (329–30). In Act III Daos brings the news of Chairestratos' feigned illness to Smikrines. To convey this news in an appropriately solemn manner, Daos takes a tragic part. He becomes what ancient grammarians called an *exangelos*, a messenger who comes from within the house to convey news to those outside. He comes from the house with a tale of woe, and he reinforces his serious pose with a string of tragic quotations. Despite the old man's impatient comments, twenty-one lines of exclamation pass before Daos breaks the news. Then he lapses into a second string of quotations, pausing only to identify the author of each. Such lengthy expression of woe is in marked contrast to the brevity of his actual message: Chairestratos is near death, he suffers from choler, pain, frenzy, and choking, Chaireas has gone for a doctor. Only some three of Daos' lines advance the action. The rest are for dramatic effect. This broad adaptation of a tragic posture is of the type familiar from Aristophanes.

Tragic motifs and devices appear constantly in Aristophanes, but always twisted and turned toward the comic. Bellerophon's winged horse becomes the giant dung-beetle of *Peace*. In the *Thesmophoriazusae* Mnesilochos appeals for help by writing his messages on votive tablets as the hero of Euripides' *Palamedes* did on oar blades, and the attempts to rescue him take the form of broad parodies of similar scenes in the *Helen* and *Andromeda*. These comic figures strike a pose not primarily to advance the action but to get a laugh by incongruous invocation of the tragic. The logic of the use and appropriateness of such parodies is the comic logic Cedric Whitman has identified as being so characteristic of the Aristophanic hero. 'The comic hero himself', he writes, 'is wayward and abides by no rules except his own, his heroism consisting largely of his infallible skill in turning everything to his own advantage, often by a mere trick of language.'[4] Euripides of the *Thesmophoriazusae* attempts a rescue by making 'life' imitate his own art, just as Dikaiopolis became Telephos because he knew the power of tragedy to sway audiences. Menander's Daos self-consciously quotes from tragedy after tragedy to overwhelm Smikrines with his affected solemnity. Two features, however, distinguish Menander's tragic burlesque. First, it is not entirely incongruous. Daos' sudden ability to quote tragedies was prefigured by his earlier identification as Kleostratos' *paidagogos* (14), and the message he brings is appropriate to the role of tragic *exangelos*.

Second, though the audience may find his display laughable, it actually *does* overwhelm Smikrines. His interspersed signs of impatience give way to expression of shock, worry, and amazement as the sudden news distracts him from the business of claiming Kleostratos' estate. Daos' entry effectively disrupts Smikrines' scheming and thus both advances the counter-plot against him and amuses the audience with its elaborately feigned solemnity.

The solemnity is then quickly followed by the gloomy pronouncements of a charlatan doctor. Chaireas had agreed to equip a friend with wig, cloak, stick, and foreign accent to play the part (376–9). This part, like that of a cook or parasite, was a familiar comic type. It may have originated in fifth-century Doric comedy; the comic doctor was certainly well known to Athenian audiences. *The Doctor* (*Iatros*) is a title attested for Antiphanes, Aristophon, Theophilos, and Philemon, and there are numerous contexts that suggest the doctor's presence.[5] Doric speech was evidently a frequent part of his characterization. In a play by Alexis called *The Girl Dosed With Mandrake* (*Mandragorizomene*, fr. 142K) a character actually complains of the respect a Doric doctor's prescriptions command solely because of his accent. Menander's doctor combines Greek comedy's enduring love of dialect humour with the solemn absurdity of such Aristophanic quacks as the petitioners to Cloudcuckooland. Having 'examined' Chairestratos he loads his speech with pompous jargon and hyper-doricisms. He has two ways to say outright that Chairestratos will not live (447, 450), but the rest of his speech is a blur of inconsistent medical observations whose incoherence is only partly due to the tattered state of our papyrus. He embroiders his prognosis with technical mumbo-jumbo while emphasizing with quick repetitions the only thing he actually wants his listener to remember. The rapid succession of burlesqued messenger and foreign doctor gives the act a distinct comic colour through the contrast between the seriousness of their message and the absurdity of their manner. Their posturing guarantees broad humour, and there is no serious undercurrent here to diminish it. These comic messengers of death make light of seriousness, but seriousness is not always treated so. The *Aspis* begins in a very different mood, and how Menander moves his play from the death march of Act ɪ to the hilarious posturing of Act ɪɪɪ is the direct result of his handling of light and serious elements we call the mixture of modes.

Daos' initial appearance is in a role quite different from his later burlesque of the tragic *exangelos*. His mournful report of a military catastrophe in Lykia opens the play with a combination of exposition and spectacle calculated to evoke the image and response of genuine tragedy. Like Sophocles' Teucer over the dead Ajax and like his Electra to the supposed funeral urn of Orestes, Daos apostrophizes the lost Kleostratos, lamenting the change of fortune that has overtaken them. His first nine lines conform to the norms of tragic metre, and his diction is in the tragic style. The line of captives and baggage that accompany him heighten the effect, and so does sight of the battered shield of the title, to which he gives considerable emphasis (15–17). When called upon to explain what has happened, Daos becomes a tragic messenger.[6] His narrative speech begins and ends with tragic formulae, and the description of Kleostratos' corpse bloated beyond recognition makes a powerful impression. But the *Aspis* is not a tragedy. Daos is accompanied by Smikrines, and while the *paidagogos* assumes a tragic stance, Smikrines remains a wholly comic type. He is named almost at once, and between his name and mask the audience could recognize the miserly old man of comedy. He interrupts the messenger's speech at regular intervals, sometimes simply to elicit further details, but at other times with character-revealing comments. He admires the war booty Daos has brought with him (33), he disapproves of the soldiers' revelry even before learning its unfortunate consequences (48, cf. Smikrines of *Epitr.* 127), and he displays the selfish man's approval of Daos' own good fortune in escaping the debacle (62). When the narrative ends, his questioning immediately centres on the booty, and his protest of disinterest is palpably false. Menander uses his words to confirm the expected image of the comic miser. Daos and Smikrines engage in a tragic–comic counterpoint that tempers the tragedy of Daos' talk with the promise of comedy to come. Daos' narrative also contains the isolated facts that will provide the true explanation of events: the enemy took prisoners, the shield was the only means of recognition, quick burial made further inquiries impossible. The material for comedy, though present, is kept in the background.

A prologue follows. The goddess Fortune (Tyche) must immediately disavow contact with anything unpleasant, and that disavowal recognizes both the tragic impact of the preceding scene and the dramatic need to assert the eventual primacy of a light mode. The first part of her speech offers a comment and perspective on the action we have witnessed (99–121). She retells Daos' story with a lighter touch the truth makes possible, and she reinforces our initial impression of Smikrines as a miser. She then passes to some necessary background information concerning what Smikrines' younger brother Chairestratos had intended for his niece and what Smikrines now intends (122–46). This scheme, which Fortune describes only in general terms, follows naturally from our understanding of his character, and the further information that his plan will fail follows naturally from our knowledge that Kleostratos is still alive. The question that remains after all these revelations is not one of what, but of how. The prologue releases the tension created by the opening scene, thus directing attention to Smikrines and his plot, which are essentially comic. The tragic–comic counterpoint begins to reverse itself, for Fortune had given the 'right' (i.e. comic) perspective on events. Her prologue is linked to the earlier action by the order of her material and to the following scene by her emphasis on Smikrines. Fortune identified him explictly as a miser (*philargyros*, 123), and when Smikrines reappears he at once explicitly denies that label (149). She described him with an emphatic string of negatives (117–19), and his first speech begins with another string (149–52). When Daos enters he discusses the scheme Fortune had sketched, and the comedy is launched.

This turn to comedy, however, is gradual. As Smikrines attempts to win Daos to his side he is met by the deferential solemnity that had characterized Daos' first appearance. When pressed for his opinion Daos resorts to the Delphic maxim 'know thyself' and a plea to be excused from judgment.

I am Phrygian. Many things that seem right
to you people seem outrageous to me, and
vice versa.   (206–8)

Daos' observation is a commonplace of fourth-century thought
that was a perennial subject for comic embellishment. In a play
by Anaxandrides, who wrote in the first half of the fourth
century, a speaker excuses himself from aiding Egyptians with
a long appeal to their different standards, beginning with the
lines,

I couldn't be your ally; neither our
customs nor our laws are in accord. They
differ from each other quite a bit.   (fr. 39K)

A speech on parasites by Nikolaos, a writer closer to Menander's own time, contains the observation,

. . . Being Phrygian he couldn't bear
the frankness of one born to it with good grace.   (fr. 1K)

The significant thing here in the *Aspis* is that Menander has
chosen *not* to embellish Daos' remark in the customary way,
and, as we shall see in a moment, this is not because Menander
particularly avoids ethnic humour. This scene is part of the
gradual modulation from the tragic solemnity that opened the
act to the broad humour that will close it. As such, too much
overt humour would be out of place. Daos' statement that he is
a Phrygian leads us to expect a joke that comes only in the
following scene, where the light mode predominates. Here
Daos ends the scene with a plaintive appeal to Fortune that, in
view of the prologue, lightens the mood for the audience by its
gentle and unconscious irony. The stage is set for an outbreak of
genuine humour.

A cook, dependable representative of comedy that he is, now
enters, full of complaints. Something is always ruining his
contracts, he says, and this time,

. . . Some corpse
has come from Lykia and swept everything away
by force.   (224–6)

His complaint is not only a comic exaggeration of the facts that makes light of the bloated corpse in Daos' opening narrative; it is a parody of precisely the kind of messenger's speech Daos had delivered so seriously. The messenger who brings the news of Xerxes' defeat at Salamis to Queen Atossa in Aeschylus' *Persians* may come to mind.

> A Greek man came from the Athenian camp
> and said the following to your son Xerxes: (*Pers.* 355–6)

Menander uses the one-dimensional cook for a laugh at the tragic posturing he had previously introduced and then has him revert to character as he directs a torrent of abuse at his assistant for failing to steal oil from the house, a stock motif of cooks' scenes.[7] He is then followed onstage by another stock figure, a caterer. Daos must again identify himself as a Phrygian, and now the ethnic humour avoided in the previous scene bursts out. The comments on Phrygian effeteness and Thracian virility were set up by the caterer's deliberate, largely gratuitous question and Daos' monosyllabic reply (241ff.). The jokes are a commonplace of comedy used here in conjunction with the stock figure of cook and caterer to end the act on a broadly comic note.[8] The first act thus moves from the tragic parade to a succession of comic types as we see the effect of Daos' news on Smikrines and the hired professionals. Daos himself is the linking figure. He is present at each step in the sequence, and his ethnicity is used first to set him apart from Smikrines and then to trigger the concluding bit of humour. He seems to be emerging as a central character in the action, but his progress is not smooth.

Smikrines attempts to take charge in Act II. He breaks the news of his plan to his brother Chairestratos with abrupt commands and an insistence on his rights. He stubbornly maintains that though he is older, he is not the 'old man' Chairestratos claims he is. Chairestratos' remonstrance is based more on a basic sense of decency than a strict sense of legality; his offer of the property to Smikrines without the girl is, as Smikrines perceives, full of legal pitfalls (264ff.). Smikrines has the facts, and they put him in command. Chairestratos is left with only a 'might have been', or so it seems. With his appeal to Smikrines as 'guardian of the family' (*kyrios*, 265) and his later remark to Chaireas that he hoped to leave Chaireas and Kleostratos as 'guardians of my estate' (*kyrioi*, 281) Menander is playing upon the double sense of the word *kyrios*. The legal concept of guardianship (*kyrieia*) forms the very basis of Smikrines' scheme, and it is to legal status that Chairestratos alludes. Yet throughout the play Menander keeps the mechanism of the law in the background. There is no mention, for example, of the public hearing required to establish Smikrines' right to claim marriage with the heiress, and the precise status of each character under the law is deliberately left vague.[9] Here the legal meaning of *kyrios* blends into the general sense of 'master' or 'superintendent', and that general sense echoes Fortune's announcement in the prologue that *she* is 'mistress of all this' (*kyria*, 147). Indeed, Chairestratos' somewhat wistful memory of his hopes and the details of his offer to Smikrines, which mention the joint upbringing of Chaireas and the girl and the dowry of two talents he was going to provide, are almost identical in language and detail with Fortune's exposition (262–9, 278?–83, cf. 128–36). This echo of the prologue reminds the audience that all will turn out well. It takes the sting out of Smikrines' cruelty and makes his insistence more foolish than fearful. The old men exit in succession, leaving the young Chaireas alone onstage to deliver a short monologue.

Chaireas addresses the absent Kleostratos much as Daos did at the opening. He bemoans the change of fortune. There is the same solemn vocative, and Chaireas even slips into four lines of tragic metre (289–92). His speech is distinctly serious in mode, and the statement that he has treated Kleostratos' sister honourably, 'having done nothing rash, or unworthy or unjust', is an explicit disavowal of the very conduct so characteristic of young men in comedy. He ends with the same remark as Chairestratos; the law threatens to dictate a different *kyrios* of these affairs. Once again, however, the echo of the prologue takes the sting out of the situation and makes it faintly amusing. The extra knowledge Fortune provided works in counterpoint with the sad complaints and Smikrines' threats to lend the act a comic undercurrent which soon breaks to the surface with Daos' shouts. Events have been too much for Chairestratos. He has collapsed within the house, and now Daos calls upon

Chaireas to help him bring the stricken man out.[10] Fortunately, Chairestratos is not so severely stricken that he cannot express his suffering in words, and he does so using stock expressions of comic distress that prevent us from taking his collapse too seriously (305–7, cf. *Dys.* 54, *Epitr.* 879). Daos now takes charge, and he uses Chairestratos' attack and his wish for death as elements of his scheme. As we have seen, the three plan together the counterplot that leads to the broad humour of Act III and the eventual foiling of Smikrines.

This scheme is central to the ensuing action. Daos hatches the plot, but he is not quite the clever slave we know from Roman Comedy. It is not his plot alone. Chaireas and Chairestratos join him in the plotting, and each makes a contribution of some significance. Chaireas, who knows no foreign doctors, volunteers a friend instead to play the part. He thus augments the element of outright fraud that will enrich the comedy of the following scene. Chairestratos, in answer to Daos' question, decides who will be informed of the plan and who will not. The language of all these characters is direct and businesslike, with none of the extravagant and colourful language that might focus attention on any one of them. The contributions of Chairestratos and Chaireas, though not essential to the scheme, nevertheless mark them as co-conspirators. Daos does not dominate this scene as his descendants in the tradition come to do. A parallel scene from Plautus makes an interesting contrast.

The slave Palaestrio opens the third act of *The Windbag Warrior* with a monologue on the importance of secrecy. He looks about him to see that the coast is clear and then somewhat peremptorily summons the old man Periplectomenus and the *adulescens* Pleusicles from Periplectomenus' house.

PA. evocabo. heus Periplectomene et Pleusicles, progredimini!

PE. ecce nos tibi oboedientes.   PA. facilest imperium in bonis.

PA. I'll summon them. Hey, Periplectomenus and Pleusicles! Come out!

PE. Here we are. Your servants.   PA. Commanding good men is easy.   (*MG* 610–11)

After an extended comic dialogue Palaestrio brings them to the matter at hand, a plan to best the soldier Pyrgopolynices and get Pleusicles' girl Philocomasium out of his clutches. Palaestrio will distract the soldier from Philocomasium with a second girl posing as Periplectomenus' wife. He demands a ring from Periplectomenus to be a love token from the 'wife' and then orders the old man off to find a suitably attractive and available girl. With Periplectomenus gone, he reminds Pleusicles to address Philocomasium as 'Dicea' from now on and promises to give further instructions when the time is right. Pleusicles then leaves the stage to Palaestrio, who ends the scene with a short monologue.

> Quantas res turbo, quantas moueo machinas!
> eripiam ego hodie concubinam militi,
> si centuriati bene sunt manuplares mei.

> What a turmoil I'm whipping up, what engines set in motion!
> Today I'll snatch away the soldier's girl,
> if only my troops are well deployed. (813–15)

Palaestrio commands. Periplectomenus and Pleusicles are his agents. This is the normal arrangement of roles in Plautus, who favours extensive scenes of plotting dominated by slaves like Palaestrio. The military language here, which is particularly appropriate to describe the campaign against Pyrgopolynices, is characteristic of many Plautine schemers. Chrysalus of *The Bacchis Girls* sings a long song in which he likens himself to the sackers of Troy, and Pseudolus uses military imagery to describe his campaign against Ballio (*Bacch.* 925–78, *Pseud.* 574–93). The language and the very length of such scenes make the Plautine slave and his intrigue central to the action.[11]

There is no comparable emphasis in extant Greek comedy. A few papyrus fragments, including a scene from Menander's *Girl from Perinthos*, certainly suggest intrigues. 'It's silliness to cheat an easy-going, empty-headed master,' says Laches in that play, probably taunting his slave with an echo of the slave's earlier boast (13–15, cf. fr. 3). An unidentified fragment from Oxyrhynchus includes a short monologue in which another Daos announces an intention to help his young master by means of a scheme. 'Daos,' he tells himself, 'now is no time to lie down on the job ... That's cowardice.'[12] Such Greek examples, however, all lack the colourful language and sheer

length that Plautus uses to mark his slaves as true controllers of
the action, nor can we ever tell how prominently these suggested intrigues actually figured in their plays. Menander's
Perinthia, for example, is one of two plays Terence claims to
have used to make his *Andria*, and Terence's slave there neither
controls the action nor seizes the limelight. In the *Aspis* Daos
determines the course of action against Smikrines, but his
cleverness is not the focus of Menander's attention. That is why
Chairestratos and Chaireas contribute to the scheme. They do
not receive their instructions with the mock servility of Periplectomenus and Pleusicles, nor does Daos close the scene with a
flamboyant monologue. His concluding lines – if Daos is indeed
the one who speaks them – simply look ahead to the developments of the next act.[13] Menander keeps the amount of stage
time devoted to planning the intrigue at a minimum. He
streamlines the scene to emphasize not the cleverness of the
schemers, but simply the details of their plan. Unlike Palaestrio, Daos does not completely upstage his masters.

Though he is an important character throughout the play as
we have it, Daos never quite dominates. The drama of his
opening scene is persistently undercut by Smikrines' remarks,
and when he later runs circles around the old man the scene is
brief and soon yields place to the comic doctor. Nor is his
characterisation strictly consistent. The broadness of his play
in Act III is in marked contrast to his initial dignity and solemnity. Daos first appeared in the role of faithful retainer, which is
frequently a colourless and even protatic role, and interest in
him came from Menander's ability to cast him in a tragic
mould with a solemnity he maintained throughout the first act.
He treated Smikrines with diffidence and that stuffy moralizing
about contrasting customs, and he played straight man to the
broad humour of cook and caterer. Then in Act II diffidence was
forgotten as he became a schemer, and in Act III he parodies
tragic *exangeloi* in a scene whose humour is as broad as that of
the cook and caterer to whom he has previously yielded place.
This movement in Daos from tragic to comic stance parallels
the play's modulation from serious to light. Menander uses the
figure of Daos as his prime agent for the mixing of modes,
allowing him to assume whatever role necessary to give the

action the desired tone. In this Daos is unique and contrasts with both the play's one-dimensional figures and the more interesting characters who nevertheless remain consistent, recognizable types. Cook and caterer generate humour by their very presence. Chaireas represents the love interest. Smikrines and Chairestratos provide comic villainy and comic bewilderment. We cannot tell what Daos will represent until we see him in action. His character is fluid and therefore of particular value to the dramatist in the making of his play.

The *Aspis* is a typical play of intrigue made unique, and therefore interesting to an audience, by its contrast of tone. Daos, as loyal attendant, intriguer, jokster, and straight man, is the vehicle for creating that contrast. As a comic slave he is not a consistent type but a composite with a new, still developing role. He represents a midpoint between Xanthias of Aristophanes' *Frogs*, who exerts a powerful but consistent influence on his play, and the later Pseudolus, a character so resilient and so commanding that he can exist beside the most memorable villain in Roman comedy and still dominate his play.[14] Menander is developing the concept of the flexible character who can alter the tone of a play by his ability to change his stance as the dramatist requires. Precedent for such a character is not to be found in extant Attic comedy; it lies in Euripides' experimentation with dramatic roles and his striving for new effects by blending familiar elements in new ways. A particularly fine example of such experimentation with roles is the Menelaos of his *Helen*.

Like Daos, Menelaos is a figure who changes modes to meet the dramatist's changing requirements, and his changes are largely responsible for a unique tone that has long perplexed the play's critics. One recent discussion refers to the *Helen*'s 'hesitation between tragedy and comedy', while another calls it 'chameleon-like, persistently shifting, in mood, verbal fabric, and the values which it implies'. At the root of these fluctuations is Menelaos. As the action unfolds, Euripides has him enact three successive situations familiar to the tragic stage, but in each case Menelaos refuses to play his part properly. He is cowardly in the type of gatekeeper scene which usually demonstrates a tragic hero's resolve (435ff.). He is ludicrous in a

potential rescue (541ff.), and his slow-wittedness almost ruins
the recognition scene with his wife (557ff.). Only the sudden
report of an old sailor, coming like a voice from the machine,
prevents him from abandoning the true Helen for the phantom
he has brought back from Troy.[15] In the great debate before the
Egyptian princess Theonoe, Euripides nearly has him step out
of character entirely. Theonoe must decide their fate, and
Menelaos is called upon to plead for her support. He begins
with a disavowal of precisely the mournful supplication that
had served him so badly before the gatekeeper. The speech he
then delivers is filled with condescension toward tragic and
heroic *topoi* and plays dangerously with the tragic mood.[16]
Menelaos thus announces his independence and distance from
the figures of high tragedy. Yet once he does so, he is prepared
to act courageously, as subsequent events indicate. The rags in
which he first appears are replaced by costly robes, and when
called to action he sweeps the Egyptians aside as he and Helen
make their escape in a stolen ship. Only this report of him at the
end fully conforms to the conduct expected of a hero.

What we find in this Menelaos is a dramatic figure of mixed
modes used for a new purpose. Though entangled in the conflict between appearance and reality that gives the play its
intellectual interest, his confusion is ludicrous rather than pro-
found, and Euripides can resolve it by the simple expedient of
the sailor's message. Nor does the treatment of his peril compare with the whirl of conflicting obligations and dangers that
surrounds Theonoe. Menelaos' eventual heroism during the
escape is the heroism of romance not tragedy, and by the time
he acts heroically offstage he has ceased to be the centre of
attention on it. The play is no more about him than Menander's *Aspis* is about Daos, but conflicts and concepts basic to the
play first arise through his presence. Like Daos, he is the vehicle
for weaving themes into the fabric of the play. Without his
implicit debasement of the heroic ideal, without his manifest
difficulty in grasping Helen's story, and without his eventual
willingness to play the romantic hero we would have a very
different play. By casting and re-casting Menelaos in a variety
of guises Euripides alters the tone of his drama and forces it
onto a new plane.

That new plane for play-making is neither tragic nor comic in the traditional sense. By stretching the conventions and the roles of his genre Euripides opened up a new range of possibilities for his successors. Daos is similar to Euripides' Menelaos not in character but in dramatic function. The *Aspis*, like the *Helen*, draws its impact from its tone. Its juxtaposition of serious and light elements creates a complex blend of modes that gives its rather mechanical intrigue unique interest and individuality. Menander's technical problem was to find a suitable vehicle for the necessary modulation from the dramatic despair that created the play's impact in the opening scene to the gaiety and exuberance necessary to enliven the intrigue and bring it to a comic climax. He found that vehicle, as Euripides did before him, in a character whose flexibility could make him at home in either mode and who, by changing his stance, could bring the audience with him in a progression from serious to light. The result is a play whose extremely successful theatricality comes from the blend of humour, pathos, and sophisticated parody made possible by the skillful mixture of modes.

Perikeiromene (The Shorn Girl):
Plot and Situation

Preserved among the anecdotes in Plutarch's *Moralia* is Menander's remark that, though the festival was approaching and his play remained unwritten, he had worked out the theme and needed only set the lines to it (*Moral.* 347e). The story reflects an emphasis on plot construction that was a legacy of Aristotelian literary theory and a hallmark of New Comedy. 'Plot', says Aristotle in a famous passage of *The Poetics* (1450a38), 'is the basic ingredient and, as it were, the soul of tragedy.' By plot (*mythos*) Aristotle means the ordering principle behind a play's action; that is why *mythos* is frequently amplified by a phrase like 'the structure of events' (e.g. 50a5, 15, 32). The skill in telling a story that Aristotle admired was an established part of the tragedian's art, but it was a comparatively late development in comedy.[1] The plot linking divergent songs, burlesques, and digressions is rarely the main attraction of Aristophanic comedy, and the emphasis on descriptive scenes such as banquets and courtships in the next generation of comic writers is more clearly linked to the later forms of mime and satiric dialogue than to subsequent drama. New Comedy, however, holds comic digressions in check and makes them serve the requirements of a narrative plot. As we have seen in the *Aspis*, Menander uses the minor characters only sparingly to highlight major characters and actions, and the self-characterizing monologues he may give a figure, though they stop the action and appear to digress, provide necessary exposition and motivation, adding credibility and interest to the action.

Yet the scope of that action seems extremely limited. It is confined to domestic matters and a small number of masks. This narrow range of setting and character is further limited by what are sometimes called 'late point-of-attack' plays. As A. W. Gomme put it, 'the Greeks were generally concerned only with the last part of the story, with the solution, not the tying of the knot; the first part was all put into a prologue or one or two exposition scenes.'[2] This tendency cuts further into the dramatist's range for plot construction. If, for example, a play is to deal with an estranged couple, emphasis falls on the effect, not the cause of the estrangement. Not only is the stock of domestic dilemma therefore limited, but the dramatist's perspective on the dilemma seems to be limited as well. How then did a writer such as Menander gain a reputation for originality in plot construction? The answer lies in a process of skillful combination. This chapter will examine how Menander combined elements and will formulate a critical vocabulary to describe his technique for making plots.

One obvious source of variety in making a play is to recast the role of a familiar comic figure, and this is what Menander does in the *Perikeiromene*. The soldier, like the cook, caterer, and physician, was a stock type, and he was generally vulgar, boastful, and dull-witted. In an unidentified fragment of Menander, for example, a character baits a pompous and slow soldier at a dinner party.

> How did you get this wound? ::
> From a javelin. :: How, in God's name? :: On a ladder
> while scaling a wall. :: I point it out
> studiously, while the others snort in derision   (fr. 745K–T)

'There couldn't be a sophisticated soldier,' runs another fragment, 'not even if God tried to make one' (fr. 554K–T). The ability to be sophisticated (*kompsos*), with its double sense of refined and clever, is a term of praise in Menander that was beyond the capabilities of the stock soldier. Bias, who played an important part in Menander's play *The Fawner* (*Kolax*), seems to have been a soldier of this type, fond of boasts about his prowess as drinker and womanizer (fr. 2, fr. 4). Polemon of the *Perikeiromene* might seem to fit this pattern as well, for he is excitable and rash. His mistress Glykera was seen in the arms of a young man she alone knows is really her brother, and in a fit of jealousy Polemon cuts off her hair. This headstrong act brings

about their estrangement, but when the action gets under way
he is a soldier who has lost his bluster.

> Our swaggering soldier of a moment ago,
> who doesn't let women keep their hair,
> has collapsed in tears over lunch.   (172–4)

This collapse of Polemon's bravado puts the soldier in a new
role. *He* becomes the sympathetic, romantic hero, while his
rival Moschion actually assumes many characteristics of the
comic soldier.

Menander's success in recasting the soldier of the
Perikeiromene is paralleled by a similar success in the *Misoumenos*,
whose Thrasonides is a model of self-restrained passion. Like
Polemon, he is a soldier cast out of his expected role by love.

> A paltry little girl has enslaved me completely,
> a thing no enemy has ever done.   (fr.2)

These similar, sympathetic soldiers figured in similar dramas.
Though the fragmentary remains of the *Misoumenos* leave crucial parts of the action unexplained and the reconciliation scene
of the *Perikeiromene* is largely lost, we can still construct a
schema that describes the sequence of actions in both plays:[3]

A soldier and a girl who are otherwise compatible have, because of a
misunderstanding, become estranged. The girl, angered and hor-
rified, separates herself, and the soldier is in despair. While separated
the girl unexpectedly discovers her missing father. As a result of this
discovery the girl's status is altered, the source of the misunderstanding is revealed, and the girl is formally betrothed to the soldier.

The pivotal incidents in this common schema are the soldier's
despair, which sets in motion the process of recognition, and
the recognition itself, which initiates the eventual reconciliation. In the *Perikeiromene* the despairing Polemon sends his
friend Pataikos to intercede for him with Glykera, and while on
this mission Pataikos discovers that Glykera is his daughter.
Thrasonides' slave Getas, frightened by his master's threats of
suicide in the *Misoumenos*, moves all the swords in the house
next door, and the sight of a certain sword there causes the
stranger Demeas to rush outside, where he is unexpectedly

reunited with his daughter, Krateia. The process of sorting out the misunderstanding then begins.

Though the recasting of the comic soldier in a sympathetic role thus provides Menander with one source of variety, his Polemon and Thrasonides share many traits and find themselves in similar predicaments. Are the *Perikeiromene* and *Misoumenos* therefore the same? Clearly not, and this ability to fashion different plays from what is ostensibly the same material requires a distinction between 'plot' and 'situation'. Care in applying these terms will enable us to identify with precision how Menander's technique of combination works to produce variety in his plays.

Strictly speaking, our schema is not the outline of a plot but a compilation of separate situations: estranged lovers, despairing hero, a recognition. Aristotle would call them *pragmata*. Such situations are by their very nature dynamic. Each is comprised of characters arranged in a particular way like chessmen on a board, and, like chessmen, they are capable of motion. As the characters move they link the situations of which they are part in a particular way. This movement from situation to situation is the actual plot, Aristotle's 'structure of events'. When Aristotle says that a play is a *mimesis* of a *praxis* he means this chain of actions.[4] What can distinguish one plot from another is the way the dramatist develops the dynamic potential of his situations, the way he forges the links. Variety in plot construction may thus be a function of the dramatist's ability to individualize his characters, not necessarily to invent new situations. We have seen that both the *Perikeiromene* and *Misoumenos* turn upon the soldier's despair and the girl's recognition. In each play, however, Menander dramatizes these situations differently, and consequently the links of each chain are distinct.

In the *Perikeiromene* Sosias prepares us to see in Polemon a picture of despair. Having left his house after the outrage, Polemon is anxious for news of Glykera, and he contrives errands for Sosias to get reports of her conduct and condition. Sosias complains of these errands as slaves in comedy often do, but he interrupts himself with an outburst of sympathy for his master that is particularly striking because of its unexpected context.

I see my master thoroughly wretched, and it's
no dream, I know. What a bitter homecoming! (359–60)

We first see this despairing figure as party to an absurd expedition against the house next door where Glykera has taken refuge (467ff.). Sosias, not Polemon, commands this expedition. An abusive exchange between Sosias and Moschion's slave Daos in the previous act had established Sosias as a low comic figure (373–97). By putting him at the head of the rabble of slaves that makes up the attack force Menander keeps Polemon one step removed from farce. We can contrast an otherwise similar scene in Terence's *Eunuch* in which the soldier Thraso organizes a similar attack to abduct a girl from another house (*Eun.* 771ff.). Thraso, a typical *miles gloriosus*, ostentatiously deploys his 'troops', carefully reserving a place for himself in the rear, and there is elaborate joking with military terms among Thraso and his followers Gnatho and Sanga. In addition to this linguistic play, the scene offers excellent opportunities for broad comic action. There is comic dialogue and spectacle in Menander's scene as well, but he keeps his soldier out of it. Only Sosias uses absurd military language, and he clears the stage with some vulgar *double entendre* jokes on sex and warfare that contrast with the serious talk between Polemon and Pataikos that follows on the now empty stage.[5]

This talk arouses further sympathy for Polemon. Pataikos begins by doing most of the talking (486–503). His calmness and common sense contrast with Polemon's agitation and simplicity. Pataikos guides him step by step, trying to make him see that, whatever he may have thought, he has no legal hold over Glykera. He has thought of her as a wife, but theirs was only a common law union. She is her own mistress. Nor do there appear to be grounds for legal action against Moschion. All this is too much for Polemon, and he bursts out in an expression of despair that abruptly alters the direction of the conversation.

Γλυκέρα με καταλέλοιπε, καταλέλοιπέ με
Γλυκέρα, Πάταικε.

Glykera has abandoned me, abandoned me
has Glykera, Pataikos. (506–7)

The strong word 'abandoned', emphasized by the striking chiasmus, replaces Pataikos' more neutral 'gone away' (ἀπελή-λυθεν, 492), and with this outburst Polemon puts his stamp on the remaining dialogue. Though his eloquence soon gives way to broken sentences, *he* now does most of the talking. His pressing desire to get Pataikos to intercede for him with Glykera sweeps the older man away. His frequent vocatives in addressing Pataikos (488, 507, 512 twice, 517, probably 524), his inability to complete a thought grammatically (507–10, 514–16), and even his self-confessed lack of control (522–23) convey his desperate desire to win his friend to his side. This honest and earnest desperation convinces the reluctant Pataikos to intercede and so, ultimately, resolves the crisis of the play.

A striking feature of this portrayal of the despairing Polemon is its total lack of militarism. Polemon's talk is of Glykera: her status, her jewelry, her physique. There is none of the bravado appropriate to the soldier, though military imagery surrounds him. We find it, perhaps not surprisingly, in his retainer Sosias, and interestingly enough, in his self-styled rival, Moschion. The goddess Agnoia (Misapprehension) had mentioned in her prologue that he is rash (*thrasys*, 151), which is frequently a soldier's trait, as is his own boasting of success with women (301–4). In the dialogue with Daos that opens the second act military vocabulary is thrown back and forth between them. Daos, who is attempting to arrange an affair for Moschion with Glykera, is willing to be treated to all the horrors of war or even to have his throat cut if he is unsuccessful. Moschion calls him his scout and the marshal of his forces. Their extravagant language is particularly amusing since they are in effect waging a campaign against a professional soldier, and they are almost consciously playing roles. Daos' grandiose talk contrasts with his apparent willingness to spend the rest of his life running a mill or a shop (277, 283).[6] When it comes to action, Moschion explicitly backs away from the hero's part. Like Terence's Thraso, he reserves a place for himself behind the lines. When Daos comes out for the second time and reports that all is not as he had first thought, that Glykera has not taken refuge with Moschion's mother to facilitate a liaison, Moschion's boastful confidence crumbles, like that of a true braggart, into abuse and impatience. Use of the soldier figure allows Menander to introduce into his play the entire complex of language and action characteristic of the military *alazon*, but he divides these features among different characters to vary their effect. Polemon keeps the simple nature and impetuosity common to his type, but by dividing the concomitant boastfulness and vulgarity among Daos, Moschion, and Sosias, Menander makes his soldier a sympathetic figure without having to sacrifice the comic potential of the *miles gloriosus*.

Motifs associated with the comic soldier are apportioned differently in the *Misoumenos*. Though the text is fragmentary and our knowledge of the plot sketchy, Menander's treatment of the despairing soldier Thrasonides nevertheless makes an instructive comparison with the *Perikeiromene*. The play opens with Thrasonides voicing his anguish to the night.

> Oh Night – yours is the greatest share of
> Love's affairs; to you are most appeals
> of love and thoughts of love addressed –
> have you ever seen another man more
> miserable? another lover more ill-starred?
> I stand here now before my own house door,
> pacing up and down the street from
> dusk 'till practically your midpoint now,
> though I could rest and have the girl I love.
> She's right inside my house, and I could
> and I want to – I'm nearly mad with
> love – and yet I don't. Better for me
> to bear the rain outside,
> shivering and calling out to you.

The continuation of this scene is our newest addition to the Menandrean corpus and comes from three scraps of papyrus identified by E. G. Turner late in 1977. The text is still tentative, but a rough outline of its action is possible.[7] Thrasonides is joined by his slave Getas, who counterbalances his lament with a comic complaint about the master who walks about on such a dog of a night as if it were midsummer. He begs Thrasonides to cease his pacing, but the soldier refuses. In an expository scene reminiscent of the dialogue between Polemon and Pataikos in the *Perikeiromene*, Thrasonides explains that he has treated his captive girl as a free woman, given her control of his household, dressed her in finery, and thought of her as a wife. Yet for some reason she now hates him. The text breaks off after about a hundred lines, but a passing remark by the later writer Arrian suggests that Thrasonides asks for a sword to kill himself and then rails at Getas for refusing to give him one (fr. 2 OCT).

The situation in which Thrasonides finds himself is thus similar in several respects to Polemon's difficulty with Glykera, and his complaint to Night follows a pattern that is identifiable in other comedies. In the prologue to Plautus' *Merchant* young Charinus refuses to tell his troubles to the Sun or Moon 'as others do in comedies' (*Merc.* 3–5). A small, unidentified papyrus from Oxyrhynchus suggests a night scene in which a young man's reverie about a girl he has thought of as a wife is interrupted by his slave Syros. A larger fragment from Antinoopolis preserves the opening of another unidentified, quite possibly Menandrean play that clearly shares features with the opening of the *Misoumenos*.[8] A young man married only five days has become estranged from his wife. Like Thrasonides he is thus the victim of a disrupted union, and he explains his plight in a short monologue. He, too, believes he is the most unfortunate of men, and he also calls on Night to witness his troubles. His subsequent juxtaposition of *philia* and *agape* (τὴν φιλοῦσαν ἠλάπ[ων, 12) in describing his feelings for his wife is similar to Thrasonides' cry as later reported by Getas, 'I adore, I love you, darling Krateia' (ἀγαπῶ, φιλῶ, Κράτεια φιλτάτη, 308). The structure of the scene may also parallel the opening of the *Misoumenos*. Like Thrasonides, the young man speaks for fifteen lines before being interrupted by a servant. The scene then changes to dialogue; young man and servant appear to discuss a box of ornaments that perhaps turned out to be birth tokens crucial to the action of the play. The opening of the *Misoumenos* also switches from monologue to dialogue with the entrance of Getas, and if Thrasonides asks for a sword to kill himself in this scene and is refused, it too includes an element (Getas' decision to remove the swords) that will prove crucial to the subsequent action. There is, however, one feature that sets Thrasonides' monologue apart. It takes the form of the lover's lament beside a closed door that is known in ancient poetry as a paraclausithyron.

Thrasonides' mention of standing in the street and of disregarding time and weather emphasize the circumstances of his exclusion in terms familiar from Greek love epigram. Though surviving examples of the lover's complaint beside the closed door are more frequent in literature after Menander, the situation is alluded to by Euripides (*Cyc.* 495–502) and Plato (*Symp.* 183a); Aristophanes both parodies the theme and dramatizes the lover's song (*Lys.* 845–979, *Eccl.* 960–76). The lovers' appeals to which Thrasonides alludes in his address to Night are common in extant Greek poetry, for example as part of the girl's song in an anonymous paraclausithyron published in 1896 as *An Alexandrian Erotic Fragment*:[9]

> Dear Stars and Lady Night who shares my love,
> convey me now to him whom Kypris
> grants me, and whom
> great Eros seized.   (11–14)

The first twist in Menander, with an irony not lost upon Thrasonides himself, is that the lover is before his own door and that his own moral scruple has put him there. This self-imposed scruple prevents the violence to the door that is the excluded lover's frequent recourse, and the resulting frustration both maddens Thrasonides and awakens our sympathy for him. The second twist comes from seeing the soldier helpless. Mask and costume probably make his profession apparent, and his stance suggests a guard duty that is evidently fruitless. Death seems to be his only recourse, and Menander uses this stock motif of the excluded lover as an important element.[10] In the *Perikeiromene* Polemon also contemplated suicide, but the threat does not prove crucial (cf. 976). Getas responded to Thrasonides' threat by moving all the swords in the house next door, thus putting a certain sword where Demeas can see it and bringing about the reunion of Demeas and Krateia that resolves the dilemma of the play.

The variation in Menander's portrayal of his soldier's despair is thus the direct result of the poses he has had each one adopt. Polemon is essentially a distraught husband, as his dialogue with Pataikos makes clear. His anguish is like that of Charisios in the *Epitrepontes*, who also bitterly regrets a hasty action and its consequences. This stance sets the action off in the direction of reconciliation by causing him to plead with Pataikos for help. Thrasonides is the excluded lover of epigram, and his threat of suicide accidentally brings him help unasked. He is as helpless as Sostratos in the *Dyskolos*, saved by a coincidence and the good offices of those around him. Though their ostensible situations are the same, the dynamics of those situations are not. Different processes – one active, one passive – lead to the second pivotal situation of each play, the recognition.

Pataikos' discovery in the *Perikeiromene* that Glykera is his daughter conforms to a familiar comic pattern for untying the dramatic knot as a full-scale, late recognition complete with birth tokens unexpectedly reunites them (768ff.). Glykera's indignation at being suspected of an intrigue with Moschion led her to abandon Polemon in the first place, and this same strength of character turns Pataikos into her agent. She realizes that the birth tokens she has kept with her may now be used most effectively to improve her position, and she recruits Pataikos to help establish her identiy (742ff.). Her calm self-possession contrasts with Pataikos' friendly scepticism and her maid Doris' near hysteria. Pataikos' willingness to inspect the tokens may be tied to his earlier agreement to have Polemon show him her jewels, for he seems to react to something he has seen before. If so, Menander is taking particular care to weave key elements of his plot (Polemon's despair and Glykera's reliance on her tokens) around the figure of Pataikos, much as he linked the sequence of actions in the *Aspis* to Daos. Once Doris brings out the tokens, the recognition itself takes its course.

Menander's writing of this scene is particularly noteworthy for its mixture of modes; the solemnity of the main dialogue between Pataikos and Glykera works in counterpoint with the comic figure of Moschion who comments, unseen by them, on the action. Pataikos and Glykera shift gradually into the tragic style. Their first lines over the tokens are still comic in language, metre, and subject as they debate whether a certain embroidered figure is a goat or a stag. As they examine figure after figure and as Pataikos becomes increasingly excited, they slip into tragic style (779ff.). Their lines, many of them in stichomythia with the padding and the formality characteristic of tragedy, observe the metrical practice of tragic iambics, and there are distinct echoes of Euripides.

πῶς οὖν ἐχωρίσθητ᾽ ἀπ᾽ ἀλλήλων δίχα;
How then were the two rent asunder?   (788)

ἐπεὶ δ᾽ ἐχωρίσθησαν ἀλλήλων δίχα
Then were the two rent asunder.
(E. fr. 484.3, *Wise Melanippe*)

ἄγριον καλύψαι πέλαγος Αἰγαίας ἁλος [τὴν ναῦν]
the cruel salty-sea Aegean hid [my ship]   (809)

ταράξω πέλαγος Αἰγαίος ἁλος.
I will shake the salty-sea Aegean.   (E. *Tro.* 88)

In line 788, however, Pataikos is talking about the separation of twins while Euripides' context is the separation of heaven and earth. Similarly, while Pataikos has lost a ship, Poseidon is announcing his intention to destroy the Greek fleet homeward bound from Troy. The subtle parody of these echoes prevents the serious moment becoming too solemn for the comic structure to bear. In his comparison of Aristophanes and Menander, Plutarch claimed that 'should the action demand something fanciful or impressive, he [Menander] opens all the stops of his instrument, as it were, and then quickly and convincingly closes them again and restores the tone to its usual quality.'[11] If this is the kind of passage he had in mind, however, Plutarch has been taken in. Menander's technique is not 'to open all the stops' but to give the impression of having done so. His language suggests the seriousness of tragedy, but he does not allow tragic solemnity to get out of hand. There is this touch of parody, and the 'usual quality' of diction is not as distant as the stichomythia is intended to suggest. Moschion's presence reminds us of that. Throughout the play Moschion has been a comic character. We know from the prologue that his hopes for a romance are based upon a misunderstanding, and this extra knowledge prevents us from taking him seriously. His dialogue with Daos at the beginning of Act II, with its play on military language and his romantic expectations, was entirely comic. In Act III his monologue changes the pace and focus by its taunts and daydreams after the serious dialogue between Polemon and Pataikos (526ff.). As an unseen witness here to the reunion of Glykera and Pataikos he again represents the light mode. The language and metre of his scattered comments are comic, and his very presence lowers the emotional temperature of the scene. But if Moschion is a comic foil, he is an especially well chosen one, for the recognition scene brings a recognition for *him* as well. He had evidently learned that he was a foundling and that he has a sister. This knowledge stimulates his desire to overhear the conversation between Pataikos and Glykera, and the ultimate reunion was a reunion *à trois* in which the comic figure of Moschion and the tragically posed girl and old man joined to end the ignorance that created the play's dilemma. The link between Polemon's despair and this reunion is forged out of Pataikos' sympathy and Glykera's strength of character. An active process of intervention and discovery welds these situations into a single plot.

The discovery of identity in the *Misoumenos* is not a full-scale recognition, for Demeas and Krateia have been separated only recently and know each other on sight. Nevertheless, the scene employs the same stylistic devices as the *Perikeiromene* recognition, though in abbreviated form. The characters occasionally slip into tragic metre (e.g. 210–15, 230–3) and there are verbal echoes of famous Euripidean recognitions (210–11 & *Helen* 557; 214–15 & *Electra* 578). Getas' inquiry into the fate of Demeas' son, where *logos* is used as a euphemism for a report of death, echoes – if the restoration is correct – Ion's questioning about the missing child of Creusa's 'friend'.[12]

εἰ] δ' οὐκ[έτ' ἔ]στι τίς λέγει σοι τὸν λόγον;
If he is no more, who gave you this report?   (246)

εἰ δ' οὐκέτ' ἔστι, τίνι τρόπῳ διεφθάρη;
If he is no more, how did he perish?   (E. *Ion* 347)

There is also the same mixture of modes. Getas' first thought when he comes upon the pair, that Demeas is Krateia's lover, is a comic error that, like Moschion's exclamations, lowers the

emotional pitch of the scene, and Demeas' sad story about the
loss of his son, which is coloured by bold and melancholy
language (e.g. 'war, the common enemy', 234), is probably
undercut by our knowledge that he is mistaken. In addition to
such similarities of technique is the similarity of function. As in
the *Perikeiromene*, the reunion of father and daughter is the first
step in resolving the dramatic dilemma. By finding Krateia,
Demeas changes her status, thus paving the way for the betrothal of girl to soldier that ends the play, and though the
process of action remains unclear in our fragmentary text,
Demeas' mission to Thrasonides to buy his daughter's freedom
probably led to the discovery of the truth about his missing son.

Both plays, then, turn on recognition scenes that share distinct stylistic features, but by altering the length and position of
the recognition in the action, Menander varies the process by
which the knot is untied. All the action of the *Perikeiromene*
culminates in Pataikos' discovery of Glykera and Moschion.
The initial estrangement came from a series of errors caused by
ignorance, and the action of the play aims at uncovering these
errors to bring about the reunion of Pataikos and his children
and the marriage of Polemon and Glykera. The prologue made
this intent explicit at the outset, and Pataikos uses the happy
reunion as a basis for the lovers' reconciliation. The recognition
scene follows the established pattern of recognition comedies
by occurring in the fourth act to resolve the complexities of the
preceding action. By simplifying the process of reunion in the
Misoumenos and putting the recognition in the *third* act, Menander restructures the sequence of actions for a different effect.[13]
The dramatic knot is only beginning to loosen. Discovery of the
sword brings Demeas and Krateia together, but its dramatic
potential has not yet been utilized fully. The truth about
Krateia's missing brother – whatever it may have been – is still
to come, as is the reconciliation and betrothal of Krateia and
Thrasonides. The play's action is less resolved by the recognition than accelerated towards a resolution. In this way the
different dynamics of the basically similar situations in the two
plays alters the shape of the action in which they figure.

One other feature of Menander's use of dramatic situations
deserves mention, and that is his avoidance of what Terence

was to call 'the double play' (*duplex comoedia, HT* 6). With the sole exception of *The Mother-in-Law* (*Hecyra*), Terence sought to enrich the action of his plays with a second pair of lovers. This tendency exists in embryo in *The Andrian Girl*, and the development of genuine double plots became a feature of his art and the main source of his success in *The Eunuch* and *The Brothers*.[14] There is no comparable development in extant Menander. In the *Perikeiromene* Moschion, whose discovery of his true identity might easily have become the focus of a second dramatic interest, is not developed as an individual. He remains an essentially shallow figure whose disparate acts serve only to initiate the main action and then move it on to its close. His presumed success with Glykera is an illusion based on his own ignorance. His comic bravado is used in counterpoint with Polemon's despair to highlight interest in the soldier. He is the comic foil to the recognition scene, though it is a serious moment for him as well. He is, in short, the subject of isolated situations used to add colour to the main action without being woven into an independent plot. The same is true of Pataikos, who aids Polemon and Glykera in turn, and whose reunion with his children serves the sole dramatic function of affecting the reconciliation that is the subject of the play. The dynamic potential of their situations does not develop independently. This technique of using characters and subordinate situations only to enrich the central action will prove significant for understanding the structure of the *Dyskolos* and *Samia*, where the opportunities for double plots are also present but not fully exploited. It will be best to speak of a variety of situations but a single plot in each play.

The value of the distinction between plot and situation should now be clear. Aristotle recognized that a play represents a chain of events and that its success depends upon the dramatist's skill in welding them into a coherent whole. Menander's tradition put at his disposal only a limited number of events to dramatize, and yet his plays exhibit great variety in their representation. The key to that variety lies in his ability to fashion new links between the common events. By distinguishing between his situations, which are standard for his genre, and his plots, which are determined by his own ordering of

them, we can articulate the source of his diversity and his reputation as a constructor of plots. Study of the *Perikeiromene* and
of its contrast with the *Misoumenos* is a test case for this distinction; the incomplete state of the texts highlights isolated elements of the chain in their fragmentary context. As we look at
more complete plays, *Dyskolos* and *Samia*, we will be able to see
how this linking of situations works to form a coherent whole.
Before doing so, however, one further point needs to be
examined: how free could Menander be to refashion familiar
elements of his tradition for new effects? The *Epitrepontes*
provides an appropriate text for examining this aspect of
Menander's art.

Epitrepontes (The Arbitrants):
The Refashioned Recognition

> To be born, or at any rate bred, in a hand-bag, whether it had handles
> or not, seems to me to display a contempt for the ordinary decencies of
> family life . . . As for the particular locality in which the hand-bag was
> found, a cloak-room at a railway station . . . could hardly be regarded
> as an assured basis for a recognized position in good society.
>
> Oscar Wilde, *The Importance of Being Earnest*

Mr Jack Worthing, abandoned in a hand-bag at Victoria
Station, is but a modern addition to a long line of foundlings in
western drama. The hand-bag which eventually effects his
recognition as Lady Bracknell's lost nephew is a descendant of
the cradle and ornaments that brought about recognition in
such plays as Sophocles' lost *Tyro* and Euripides' *Ion*, and like
Neleus, Pelias, and Ion, the recognition enables him to sur-
mount the irregularities of his upbringing and assume his
rightful position. Aristotle appreciated the usefulness of such
recognitions for making plots. In Chapter 11 of *The Poetics* he
discusses recognition (*anagnorisis*) and reversal (*peripeteia*) as
special cases of the change in events (*metabole*) upon which a
dramatic action depends.[1] A precise definition of *anagnorisis* is
hindered by the term's applicability to both the recognition of
people and the realisation of circumstances, but the tendency of
drama, as Aristotle saw, is to centre recognitions on people. In
Sophocles' *Women of Trachis* Deianeira realizes she has dipped a
robe in poison and Herakles realizes that the centaur Nessos is
the agent of his destruction, but the other recognitions in extant
tragedy are of people: Oedipus and Jocasta, Ion and Creusa,
Electra and Orestes, etc. Peripety is a change in the course of
action, while the recognition is a change in a character's
awareness of what the action means. Aristotle believed the
most dramatically successful recognition to be the type com-

bined with a peripety, for it is best integrated into the plot and action. The wide range of forms and positions a recognition can take, however, enables it to serve a variety of functions in a play. An early recognition in the *Helen* sets the action in motion; in Aeschylus' *Libation Bearers* it is actually part of the initial exposition. The double recognition of Euripides' *Iphigenia at Tauris* is one step in the development of the plot. In *Ion* a late recognition is the dénouement; in *Oedipus the King* it is the shattering climax.[2] In all these cases the object of the recognition is also a central figure in the action, for in this way recognition is most powerfully combined with peripety.

An ancient life of Aristophanes credits him with introducing the recognition scene to comedy in his lost *Kokalos*, produced sometime after 388.[3] We can, however, look as far back as *The Knights*, for Paphlagon's acknowledgment of the Sausage-Seller as his divinely ordained successor lampoons the form and language of a tragic *anagnorisis* (*Eq.* 1229–53). The emergence of the fatal oracle, like the existence of birth tokens, has been carefully foreshadowed. Its discovery initiated the action (125ff.), and a contest of oracles figured prominently in the *agon* (997ff.). Now Paphlagon questions the Sausage-Seller gruffly, much as Euripides' *Ion* challenges Creusa to identify his cradle and ornaments. To make the tragic device unmistakable, Aristophanes writes the scene almost entirely in tragic trimeters, and his observance of tragedy's metrical norms allows him both to burlesque its solemnity and to accommodate an echo of the *Alcestis* (1251–2, cf. *Alc.* 181–2), a line of Sophocles (1248), and, according to an ancient annotator, lines from Euripides' lost *Telephos* (1236, 1240) and *Bellerophon* (1249). He also heightens the comic effect by reversing the normal progress of a recognition scene. This one ends not with a reunion but with a separation as Paphlagon leaves the stage for good, and the humour depends upon the incongruity of tragic diction and posture affected by these two low characters. It is a parody of the typical Aristophanic sort, but it also fulfils a necessary dramatic function, the final rout of Paphlagon. In later comedies – and this may be why the ancient biographer settles on the *Kokalos* – the functional value of the recognition in the dramatic structure surpasses its value as a comic target. The recognition scene of

Menander's *Perikeiromene*, for example, is crucial to the action and is without trace of parody, even though it, too, is written in tragic trimeters and may remind us of Euripides' *Ion*.

The mechanics of recognition as developed in comedy after Aristophanes follows the basic tragic model, but with less variety; the recognition is generally a device to bring about the final *metabole*. A late recognition becomes the favourite mechanism for the happy ending, usually by having a lost child grown to adulthood recognized in time to effect a desired marriage or to resolve a complex dilemma. Glykera's reunion with her father and brother in the *Perikeiromene* leads to the resolution of her difficulty with Polemon; a similar reunion of parent and child perhaps climaxed Menander's *Hero*. Marriages are made possibly by late recognitions in Terence's *Andrian Girl*, *Self-Punisher*, and *Eunuch* (all based upon Menandrean originals), and in plays as diverse and late in the tradition as Molière's *Miser* and, of course, *The Importance of Being Earnest*. Such comic recognitions have three basic characteristics: they occur late but are often elaborately foreshadowed, the object of the recognition is a central character in the play, and they make possible the happy ending while drawing together any loose ends of plot. The brilliantly constructed recognition of the *Epitrepontes* refuses to fit this basic comic pattern. The recognition comes early with Onesimos' discovery of a ring in Act II. The abandoned child is scarcely more animate an object than the token. It is not a main character in the play, and the arbitration scene in which it figures does not appear to be central to the action.[4] The recognition motif wears a new face in the *Epitrepontes*, and what Menander has done to it in creating this extremely successful play is a measure of his ability to re-work a familiar element of his tradition. This chapter will examine the diverse elements that give the play its interest and will show how, by refashioning the recognition motif, Menander unites them in a coherent whole.

Like the *Perikeiromene*, *Misoumenos*, and *Samia*, the *Epitrepontes* is a play about a disrupted relationship. Charisios has learned that his wife bore a child five months after their marriage. Full of moral indignation, he moves next door and hires a harp girl to amuse himself and his friends. This is the initial situation, and the first three acts give a variety of perspectives on it. Our fragmentary knowledge of Act I suggests that the play opened with an expository dialogue between Charisios' slave Onesimos and a cook. A divine prologue may well have followed to add the further information that Charisios himself is father of the child. Such exposition was probably neutral in tone. Menander's divine prologues generally avoid passing judgment on romantic heroes, and the officious and self-centred Onesimos probably revealed more about himself than his master.[5] A more complete text begins toward the end of the act with the appearance of Charisios' father-in-law, Smikrines. Like his namesake in the *Aspis*, he is a tight and hardnosed old man. He has heard rumours of Charisios' conduct and has come to reclaim his dowry and his daughter if the reports are true. Smikrines' complaint attributes a gross extravagance and moral dissipation to Charisios that is tempered only by the audience's identification of Smikrines as a comic type generally found to be in the wrong. In Act II, still smarting under the injustice Charisios has done him, he is called upon to arbitrate another claim of injustice. His decision about the child and the ornaments leads to Onesimos' recognition of the ring among the tokens as belonging to Charisios and thence to the developments of Act III.

Two different views of Charisios are presented almost simultaneously in this act. The harp girl Habrotonon gives an account of Charisios' present conduct that undercuts the picture of debauchery painted by Smikrines. It turns out that Charisios has barely noticed her, and her speech is full of bewilderment and sympathy for the young man (436–41). While on-stage she then hears a conversation between Onesimos and the charcoal-burner Syriskos about the child and the ring. Onesimos' blunt acceptance of the fact that his master has raped a girl at the festival of the Tauropolia undercuts the moral outrage Charisios has affected toward his wife.[6] To this point the dramatic action involving the discovery of the ring and the action involving Charisios' keeping of Habrotonon developed independently, but having overheard this conversation, Habrotonon makes a connection. She was present at the Tauropolia and devises a scheme to confirm Charisios' fatherhood and to discover the girl's mother. Her intervention here leads to the resolution of the marital crisis in Act IV.

A striking aspect of the construction of the *Epitrepontes* is that the principal characters of all this action appear only briefly in the fourth act. Their drama is acted out largely by surrogates, and the most lively of these is Habrotonon. Her entrance in Act III marks her emergence as a major figure. Juxtaposed against Onesimos' mundane and self-centred concern about the ring, her speech is full of colourful and arresting language.[7] Her reference to the Panathenaia and her 'chaste marriage' with the uninterested Charisios shows wit, and her frequent use of *talas* as exclamation and adjective helps establish certain mannerisms in her diction. The speech calls attention not only to the liveliness of her mind, but to her genuine puzzlement and concern for Charisios where a cynical callousness might be more expected. The pace of the scene is kept rapid by interlocking the independent speeches of Habrotonon and Onesimos with mid-line changes of speaker. The device is then used to introduce Syriskos, and Habrotonon momentarily steps into the background to overhear their conversation. The story of the child awakens her curiosity and her sympathy. Once Syriskos leaves she is full of questions. Her first word is of the child, and only after and by means of this expression of disinterested concern does her active mind begin to absorb the details and does she realize the advantage intervention may bring her.

What begins as a questioning of Onesimos soon becomes an opportunity for Habrotonon to tell her own story about the Tauropolia, and her own personality begins to dominate the scene. She is quick to connect events and to take charge. As she does so the colourful diction that directed attention to her in her opening monologue gives way to more colloquial language. Though it is common for Menander to use characteristic mannerisms of speech to differentiate among characters, particularly striking language may be turned on and off as the dramatic emphasis requires.[8] Here the content of Habrotonon's narrative takes precedence over its style. Immediately afterward, however, as she explains her projected course of action, the language again becomes theatrical. She acts out what she will say to Charisios in a lively speech broken only by half-lines of encouragement from Onesimos (516ff.). Habrotonon will affect a role, and she gives Onesimos a sample of the lines she will speak. She will make the unknown girl's story her own, being careful to avoid errors of detail. There will be pity for herself, a flattering awe of Charisios' power, and then the news of a child. Onesimos is all admiration for her cleverness. This deliberate acting-out of her part gives Habrotonon ample scope for embellishing her words with elaborate gestures and vocal mimickry, and the performance is a brilliant example of her ability to play a role and to manipulate a man. This gift of mimickry and pretence recalls her profession and her condition. Onesimos himself points out how much she has to gain by this scheme (538–40). Yet Habrotonon's desire for freedom is only part of her motivation. Her sympathy for Charisios and the child established a less commercial side of her nature revealed before any thought of gain was introduced, and Menander has written her scene with wit and an endearing grace to arouse genuine interest in her. Practical considerations and a basic womanly sympathy are carefully combined, for she is more to the play than the harp girl standing between Charisios and his wife. By her concern for domestic arrangements and the welfare of an unknown girl and child she comes to represent *the* feminine perspective in the play. In this drama acted out through surrogates, she is the surrogate for Charisios' wife, Pamphile. The interest and complexity of her character threaten to turn the third act into a miniature drama of her own, however, and to blur the true focus of the play. To prevent this Menander changes the tone and introduces his male surrogate, Smikrines.

Unlike Habrotonon, whose role in the action is determined by a complex blend of altruism and self-interest, Smikrines' singleminded concern for his daughter's domestic affairs is the direct result of a parsimony natural to his type. He enters the play as the abusive and miserly old man of comedy. This miserliness is made clear at the outset by his complaints against Charisios: the young man buys wine at one obol the half-pint (130), he is making free with a dowry of four talents (134), he pays twelve drachmas a day for a harp girl (136). The main complaint, that Charisios has abandoned his wife (136), is wedged among these financial considerations ranging from the petty (one obol is not an outrageous price) to the genuine (four talents is indeed a substantial dowry). Yet he does not rush into a course of action. Smikrines is neither a fool nor a villain. He has come seeking further information, and his plan of attack will depend upon that investigation. Smikrines' effort to discover the true state of affairs will require the full five acts, enabling Menander to use his presence to link a variety of actions and to serve a variety of functions. Until the climax in Act IV his single-minded quest sharpens the dramatic focus on Charisios and Pamphile for the audience, and after the revelations of that act bring about their reconciliation his delayed enlightenment constitutes the dénouement of Act V.

This ability to represent the disrupted union motif to the audience motivates his appearance at the end of the third act. Just when interest in Habrotonon was beginning to direct undue attention toward her, Smikrines' appearance reminds us once again of his daughter's plight. Habrotonon had gone to carry out her plan. Onesimos flees at Smikrines' approach. The old man enters an empty stage and, judging from the remnants of his monologue, commences a bitter attack on his son-in-law (582ff.). But Smikrines is soon joined by a cook full of the usual complaints about his treatment within. The introduction of the comic cook with the attendant combination of modes prevents us from taking Smikrines and his attack too seriously. Our knowledge of the true situation has perhaps made his complaints amusing all along, and the cook's presence now augments that amusement. When Smikrines decides to take Pamphile home because Habrotonon has apparently borne Charisios' child, his error makes his increasing rage ridiculous. We soon see him attempt to put his resolve into practice. Smikrines and Pamphile open Act IV arguing about his proposal. At least part of Smikrines' appeal to his daughter is based upon the financial pettiness that had characterized his first appearance, and the absurdity of his speech probably contrasted with the decorum, honesty, and sense of Pamphile's lost reply.[9] As in Act III, where Smikrines' appearance served as a device for bringing the action round again to Charisios and Pamphile, so here he is used to bring Pamphile on-stage and to motivate what was probably a self-characterizing speech for her. The scene was necessary to allow Habrotonon to see her and to have Charisios overhear her. Smikrines is the catalyst. But perhaps the most interesting use of Smikrines as surrogate and catalyst is in the famous arbitration scene of Act II.

The arbitration scene has a double appeal. There is the comic irony of Smikrines' unknowing judgement on his grandson's fate, and there is a certain brilliance to the speeches themselves which lends the scene an independent interest of its own. The action follows a common Attic pattern for private arbitrations, but is couched in deliberately general terms, while the speeches themselves, though they contain numerous rhetorical figures, conform to the requisites of legal oratory in only a casual and general way.[10] As much emphasis is placed on the characters of the litigants as on the specifics of their arguments. Daos is surly, selfish, and dense. He had found the child and ornaments and is now claiming a right to keep the ornaments without the child, but his narrative does not distinguish between what is important and will help his case (e.g. that he alone found the child) and what is trivial or even damaging to him (e.g. his second thoughts about rearing the child because of the expense). Syriskos, who has taken the child and is now laying claim to the ornaments as well, is shrewd, articulate, and aggressive.[11] He is the one to propose arbitration, and he is able to construct a clear and appealing case. He admits the truth of Daos' account where it will not hurt him. He assumes the role of guardian (*kyrios*) for the child, thus avoiding charges of greed and making effective use of the helpless infant, which his wife is holding there in her arms (302ff.). He has a flair for the dramatic combined with suitable self-restraint. Thus his allusion to the story of Neleus and Pelias is sufficiently subtle to make his point, to impress Smikrines with his erudition while complimenting the old man on his own for recognizing the point, and to remind the audience of the possible significance of birth tokens. Smikrines' eventual decision in favour of the *child* is a measure of Syriskos' success in phrasing his case in this way. The decision, made solely on the basis of information Daos and Syriskos supply, makes the scene entirely self-contained. Only Smikrines' presence links their argument with the preceding scene. Despite the subtle writing, the scene is of very little concrete significance. The net effect of these one hundred-and-fifty lines of brilliant dramatic writing is merely to get a ring out where Onesimos can see it. The scene plays with the audience's expectations by introducing the carefully delineated characters of Daos and Syriskos only to let them fade from view and by setting up a potential recognition of the child by Smikrines that, like the first encounter of Ion and Creusa, comes to nothing. Smikrines departs none the wiser, and the child's significance is pre-empted by that of the ring. A situation rich in character and potential action here makes only a minimal contribution to furthering the plot. The oddity becomes even more noteworthy when contrasted with similar situations elsewhere.

In the fourth act of Plautus' play *The Rope* (*Rudens*) the fisherman Gripus catches a trunk in his net and is about to drag the prize home when Trachalio, claiming to know the rightful owner, gets into a tug-of-war with Gripus for its possession. Trachalio proposes arbitration and Gripus, seeing what he thinks is his opportunity, tricks Trachalio into bringing the matter before his own master, Daemones. The resulting arbitration, which brings to light the birth tokens that reunite Daemones with his lost daughter, resembles Menander's arbitration in several particulars (*Rud.* 1052ff.). Though the actual arbitration is conducted as a three-way dialogue rather than as a series of speeches, the litigants' characterizations are much like those of the *Epitrepontes*. Gripus, like Daos, is the finder of the treasure, and he is equally secretive, greedy, and surly. When Daemones proves to be a less prejudiced judge than Gripus had expected, he becomes abusive and rests his case solely on the basis of his single-handed find, thus missing the point of the dispute much as Daos did. Trachalio is more articulate and, like Syriskos, claims to represent not his own interests but those of the rightful owner. Daemones is impressed by Trachalio's argument, and the dispute is finally resolved when Palaestra appears and, in a scene reminiscent of the *Ion*, recognizes the basket in Gripus' trunk as her own and is able to identify the tokens in it one by one. The reunion of father and daughter follows immediately, and the tokens are largely forgotten as the two embrace. The recognition made possible by Daemones' arbitration thus follows the expected comic pattern. It comes late in the play to resolve the dilemma directly. Palaestra is a real presence, and the play revolves around her rediscovery of a father, reunion with a lover, and escape from a pimp. There is, to use Aristotle's terminology, an *anagnorisis* immediately followed by a *peripeteia*.

Terence's *Mother-in-Law* (*Hecyra*), where a recognition also reunites an estranged couple, offers a parallel of a different sort. Once young Pamphilus learns his wife Philumena is in a suspiciously advanced state of pregnancy, he refuses to take her back, and his father fears he may return to the hetaira Bacchis with whom he had previously spent his time. In order to convince the families that this is not the case, Bacchis agrees to visit Philumena, and while there Philumena's mother recognizes a ring Bacchis is wearing as one Philumena lost on the night she was attacked. Bacchis had received the ring from Pamphilus, and she quickly perceives the connection (816–40). The recognition effected by the ring and the hetaira's intervention resolves the dilemma much as Habrotonon's actions do in the *Epitrepontes*, but the structure of *The Mother-in-Law* is quite different. Pamphilus acts out his own drama, and the play's secondary interest is on the effect of the estrangement upon Sostrata, the mother-in-law of the title, rather than on the hetaira. The recognition, briefly recounted in Bacchis' monologue, comes only as a late and necessary device for resolving the problem.[12] It too functions in the usual way. In the *Epitrepontes* that function is altered.

The key to this altered function lies in the way Menander integrates the motif into the framework of his play. Dramatists often foreshadow a recognition with scattered hints. In *The Rope* Palaestra's concern for her lost tokens (388), Daemones' dream about a monkey and swallows (593ff.), and Trachalio's claim that the girl is Athenian (739) all prefigure the eventual recognition. In *The Miser* Molière's Valère makes scattered references to a secret about his true identity, and the mention of Jack Worthing's hand-bag in the first act primes the audience for its triumphant appearance in the last. There are more scattered hints in the *Epitrepontes*. Each separate step in the progress toward recognition is elaborately embroidered. Discovery of the ring in Act II is linked to the long and brilliant arbitration scene. Identification of its owner in Act III is tied to the emerging figure of Habrotonon and her personal drama. The recognitions of Act IV which reunite Charisios and Pamphile are brought about through dialogue with Habrotonon, and the final act deals exclusively with Habrotonon and with the bringing of the news to Smikrines. The resulting texture of variant perspectives and unique individuals is thus skillfully interlaced by the connecting thread of the recognition motif. The purpose of this rich texture is to provide the material for the dramatization of a subtle, psychological peripety brought about by the recognition. Though such peripeties as those of Oedipus and Ion also have deep psychological impact, tragic reversals are equally and invariably marked by accompanying grand and theatrical alterations of physical circumstances: Jocasta dead and Oedipus blind, Ion saved from murdering his mother. The slender Muse of Menander's domestic comedy cannot sustain such dramatic alterations, nor does the limited range of his material give much opportunity for this kind of theatricality. The outward alterations the genre permits are fixed, and so Menander gives his play depth by using them to point the way toward inner, more individualised peripeties. The significant recognition of the *Epitrepontes* is of something more basic than the parentage of an infant, and that is why the child itself is kept in the background. The hidden truth of real significance in this play is a moral one, and it is Charisios who has the revelation.

Charisios' appearance is carefully orchestrated. Act IV opens with the scene of confrontation between Smikrines and Pamphile and is followed by a dialogue between Pamphile and Habrotonon in which Charisios' paternity of his wife's child is revealed. These scenes fasten attention squarely on the absent Charisios, and the colourful monologue of Onesimos that follows emphasizes that focus. Charisios overheard Pamphile's reply to her father, and the contrast between his own priggish outrage at her fault and her modest acceptance of his quite overwhelms him.

He's a bit mad. By Apollo, he *is* mad.
He's really gone mad. He's mad, by the gods.   (878–9)

Only after this elaborate preparation does Charisios appear, and he confirms Onesimos' account in a monologue charged with emotion (908–32). Pamphile's conduct has led him to see the absurdity of his moral posturing, and his realization is all the more compelling because he is still unaware of the latest development. Charisios' forgiveness comes from within himself, not from the changed circumstances. Rationing out the material of the recognition now enables Menander to add psychological depth to his character by depicting his reaction to events in a kind of slow motion. Only once Charisios is sufficiently humble does Habrotonon appear to complete the prospective reconciliation by telling him the full truth. His revelation thus comes in two parts: recognition of Pamphile's true character and his own, followed by the discovery that their two faults are really one. Lest impact of Charisios' lesson become too powerful for the comic structure, however, Menander lightens the seriousness of this internal recognition by subtle play on the inherent improbability of the outer one.

Use of the recognition motif in the play is consistently double-edged. Syriskos' early reference to Neleus and Pelias reminds us not only of the potential significance of birth tokens, but of the fact that they are elements of myth and drama. It is hardly surprising that Charisios should be at first hard to persuade of his paternity, and so is Smikrines. When Onesimos, who brings the old man the news, quotes from Euripides' *Auge* to the effect that women were made to bear children, his quotation is as two-sided as Syriskos' allusion, and his use of the technical term *anagnorismos* is a subtle allusion to the artifice of the situation (1123–4, 1121, cf. *Poetics* 1452a16). Smikrines finally realizes that his daughter has borne an illegitimate child, but he is slower to grasp the fact that Charisios is its father. As in the earlier dialogue between Charisios and Habrotonon, the essential improbability of the fact makes possible a gradual, incredulous enlightenment calculated to amuse the more knowledgeable audience. Menander uses the dichotomy between his characters' ignorance and his audience's knowledge for a subtle play upon the dramatic illusion without quite breaking it.[13] He teases humour out of the situation to counterbalance the seriousness of the experience Charisios has undergone.

Aristotle, of course, perceived the value of *anagnorisis* as more than simply a technical device. 'Its *raison d' être*', comments Gerald Else, 'is its power to concentrate an intense emotional charge upon a single event, a change of awareness; for in that *metabole* the whole depth of a human tragedy can be "contained".'[14] Comic recognitions such as Jack Worthing's tend to shine with a spark of wit rather than a full emotional charge. In the *Epitrepontes* Menander chooses to utilize the emotional potential more characteristic of tragedy, and his technical problem then becomes one of manipulating his comic structure to support his seriousness. He solves the problem by reworking the elements of his device to keep the inner, serious change of awareness surrounded by the joyous circumstances of the external discovery. He reduces the actual object of the recognition, the child, to an inanimate bundle in the arms of Syriskos' wife, thus moving attention from the child to the impact of the child's recognition upon Charisios, and he distributes the steps in the process of recognition and realization among the acts to maximize opportunities for expanding their effects upon his characters while maintaining an underlying unity. The result is a play as rich in texture as it is original in structure.

Dyskolos (The Grouch):
A Play of Combinations

Κνήμων, ἀπάνθρωπός τις ἄνθρωπος σφόδρα
καὶ δύσκολος πρὸς ἅπαντας, οὐ χαίρων τ᾽ ὄχλῳ. . .

Knemon, a thoroughly inhuman human, and
a grouch to all. He doesn't welcome crowds . . .   (6–7)

The rhetorical flourish with which Pan introduces Knemon is
calculated to suggest a familiar figure, for the misanthrope was
an established comic type by Menander's time with a traditional vocabulary to describe his misanthropy. Pan tells us
that he lives alone, though a daughter and servant actually
share his house, and his character is much like that of
Phrynichos' *Loner* (*Monotropos*, fr.18K), who lived 'Timon's life,
wifeless, slaveless, sharp-tempered, approachless, humourless,
with my own opinions.' Phrynichos' play was produced in 414
BC, a century before Menander's *Dyskolos*; in the generation
before Menander, Antiphanes had written a *Timon* and *The
Vice-hater* (*Misoponeros*) and Mnesimachos wrote a *Dyskolos*,
while the title *Monotropos* is attributed to both Ophelion and
Anaxilas. The rural setting Pan stresses at the outset is itself
part of the characterization that types Knemon. A play by
Pherekrates called *The Rustics* (*Agrioi*) had a chorus of misan-
thropic farmers, and Menander's second *Brothers*, the original
of Terence's play of that title, presented a gruff and unsociable
farmer.

I'm a farmer, a workman sullen, bitter,
and tight.   (fr. 11K–T, cf. Terence, *Ad.* 866–7)

Such misanthropy is also evident in a fragment of Menander's
Waterpot (*Hydria*, fr. 401K–T), where a hatred of crowds and a

praise of modest country ways are familiar both in sentiment and vocabulary.

> How sweet to one who hates low ways is
> solitude, and sweet to one who practices no
> evil is the proper care of his own land.
> From crowds comes envy and the luxury
> that, flashing through the city, never lasts.

Knemon, too, is a vice-hater (388, cf. 447ff., 743–5), and his love of solitude, repeatedly stressed, is his undoing (169, 222, 597). Pan's *apanthropos* and *dyskolos* are thus key words for introducing the comic misanthrope, as are the joke about hating crowds and the insistence that Knemon lives alone.[1]

Such a character offers the dramatist certain distinct possibilities.[2] Because the misanthrope is unapproachable, other characters will fail in attempts to communicate with him. These failures, which can be dramatized with endless variety, provide a rich vein of humour. Thus Pyrrhias reports his aborted effort to make contact with Knemon (103ff.), we see Sostratos frustrated in a similar attempt (145ff.), and we watch the more boisterous Getas and Sikon fail in succession (454ff.). Secondly, because he is an obstructor fated by the very nature of comedy to be defeated, we can enjoy the eventual triumph over him. Knemon's rescue from the well will cut the dramatic knot by teaching him the need for contact with others, but the play does not end with a touching change of heart. Humour returns with the farcical torment of Knemon by Getas and Sikon in a musical fantasia based upon Knemon's unsociable disposition and the earlier scenes of asking at the door. Yet the misanthrope also teeters on the brink of seriousness. The apparent retreat of Molière's Alceste is more impressive than the wedding of comparative nonentitites that closes his *Misanthrope*; Shakespeare's Timon takes his hatred with him to the grave. Knemon, too, is a figure with some claim to poignancy. His complaints sometimes turn to self-pity, and beneath his bluster are hints of an inability to cope that peaks in the long monologue upon which the play's romantic interest and the resolution of its tension depend. The *dyskolos* figure has two sides: Menander uses both as he builds a play up around him.

His structural principle is the same one used to such great effect in the *Epitrepontes*; he keeps the central figure at a distance and develops his character indirectly. Knemon appears only briefly in Act I and intermittently in Act III. His two major scenes are in Act IV and Act V, which correspond to the climax and dénouement. Menander rations out the effect the *dyskolos* can produce as the play develops a set of situations to which he must respond. Sostratos' romance, the sacrifice to Pan, and the lost pot are separate events welded into a plot by the cumulative challenge they make to Knemon, and each situation is enacted by a different set of characters. Sostratos and Gorgias represent the love interest. Getas and Sikon develop the sacrifice motif, and the lost pot involves Knemon's immediate household. There are no continuous surrogates such as Habrotonon and Smikrines to weave these situations together. Instead, Menander uses the figure of the *dyskolos* himself, having each set of characters develop its situation as an approach to him. Approaching Knemon is both the play's chief source of humour and its basic structural device. Action develops through the process of working up to such approaches. To make the 'working up' dramatic Menander uses various minor figures. Some, such as Chaireas and Pyrrhias, vanish after a single scene. Others, such as Daos and Simiche, make more than one appearance but remain utility figures rather than significant characters in their own right. As a group they introduce the action and influence our perceptions of it without either overshadowing or overexposing the central figure. This tendency to keep Knemon in the background makes Menander's handling of minor characters particularly significant.

Pan is the first such character, chosen to put space between audience and actors. His call in the play's first line to imagine the scene emphasizes its fanciful quality, and he ends with a formulaic appeal for the audience's favour. Within this deliberately artificial frame Pan introduces themes rather then specifics. He describes Knemon at some length to type and awaken interest in him, but he mentions other characters much more briefly and gives only a hint of the direction the play's action will take. By giving and holding back information, by grammatical subordinations, and by persistent banter he establishes

certain priorities among characters without actually saying
much about them. How this play of misanthropy and romance
will develop is left unstated. Nevertheless, the introduction of
Knemon in familiar terms arouses certain expectations, and
the hint of divine influence guarantees both that events will end
happily and that the audience will not take them at face value.[3]

Action begins with the entry of Sostratos and Chaireas.
Chaireas' first words are the expository question common to
many such introductory scenes, and their conversation is
intended to furnish details Pan has omitted.[4] As a protatic
maker of leading questions and brief comments Chaireas would
be entirely colourless were it not for a single monologue which
gives him dramatic identity (57–68). His offer of help no matter
what the situation is, with its parataxis and vivid present
tenses, the characteristic speech of the parasite or fawner. Like
Habrotonon's explanation in the *Epitrepontes* of how she will
show the ring to Charisios, its lively structure introduces into
an expository scene the opportunity for mimickry and elaborate gestures. Menander uses the speech to relieve the tedium
of expository dialogue, and he spices the discussion by opening
it *in medias res*. The entrance of Pyrrhias then fills the gap, while
his description of Knemon looks ahead to the confrontation
that follows. Pyrrhias, too, is a figure coloured only by his
identification as a familiar comic type, the running slave. Like
his Roman descendants, he urges all to get out of his way, he is
practically breathless, and he is slow in making his report.[5] As
Pyrrhias appears, Chaireas begins to fade out, and both flee
before the approaching Knemon, never to return.[6] They exist
only to enliven the exposition by making it a dialogue and,
more subtly, to demonstrate certain points about Sostratos.

This scene with Chaireas and Pyrrhias presents Sostratos
with certain choices, and, as Aristotle argued, it is through
choices that character is both shaped and revealed.[7] At the
outset Sostratos does not appear very self-reliant. He seeks to
involve Chaireas in the affair because he wants a helper of
experience, and he sent Pyrrhias to make the first contact
rather than go himself. But he is quickly shown to be decent and
honest at heart. His distaste for Chaireas' unprincipled advice
reflects well on him, and he is quick to admit possible error in

sending Pyrrhias. When the terrified Pyrrhias appears and urges flight, Sostratos seems steadfast; 'you're talking nonsense' is his only reply to Pyrrhias' repeated requests to flee (123). When Chaireas is sufficiently frightened to desert the cause, Sostratos recognizes his reasons for the excuse they are. The young man thus seems possessed of both courage and good sense, perhaps only slightly undercut by our knowledge that Pan has inspired him. When measured against Chaireas and Pyrrhias his good qualities emerge clearly, but we get a different view when we see him matched against Knemon.

We have had two views of Knemon so far. Pan provided the particulars of his situation and typed him as the proverbial *dyskolos*. By telling us more about him than the other characters know, he enables us to feel superior to and remote from them. We smile at Sostratos' naïveté in thinking he can arrange a marriage without difficulty, and we wink knowingly at Pyrrhias' description of the apparent madman who answered his polite overtures with a shower of clods, stones, and wild pears. While Pan's description was a direct and omniscient narrative, Pyrrhias' account gains impetus by its confused, pre-eminently human perspective. It is accompanied by Chaireas' and Sostratos' reactions and includes extracts from the aborted conversation itself. This use of *oratio recta* to enliven a report became a standard technique for Menander, for example in the *Samia* to spice a crucial narrative (206ff.) and in the *Sikyonios* to heighten the effect of a messenger's long speech (176ff.). Here in the *Dyskolos* the device makes the scene on the hill come alive, underscoring the source of Pyrrhias' terror and looking to the entry of Knemon in hot pursuit. The description actually makes Pyrrhias' conduct sound more sensible than Sostratos' anger at his failure, and it is confirmed by Sostratos' own conduct once his friends desert and he faces the raging *dyskolos* alone. He promptly backs down, just as Pyrrhias had urged.

Knemon's entrance has been carefully prepared, for both prologue and exposition look forward to this moment. Pyrrhias announced his imminent arrival nine lines before he actually reaches the stage, and Sostratos follows his progress up the *parodos* with uneasy comments. Knemon threatens, he shouts, and of course he walks alone (147ff.). His appearance was no

doubt striking – it clearly frightens Sostratos – and his monologue is equally so. Its content is just what we expect. He
alludes to the encounter Pyrrhias has just described, and his
complaint about the crowd echoes Pan's joke in the prologue.
The sardonic reference to Perseus, though not without comic
parallels, is both startling and amusing.[8] Knemon wants a
winged horse and a Gorgon's head, but by naming Perseus
outright and only alluding to the objects he implies a different
wish, to be Perseus himself. The contrasts between irascible old
man and mythological hero and between grandiose wish and
trivial complaint are both unexpected and comic. But the
speech has rather a different effect upon Sostratos. Despite his
heroic resolve, Sostratos' only thought now is for his own safety.
Overwhelmed by the ferocious appearance, extravagant language, and heavy sarcasm of the old man, he speaks only a
feeble excuse, and that a false one, for his presence. Menander
denies him a satisfactory exchange, and his only decision is to
get additional help. He had sought Chaireas thinking him
experienced in such matters; now he will find his slave Getas,
who is a man of the world (184). Sostratos remains dependent
on others. The impression of maturity and resolution created
by the exchanges with Chaireas and Pyrrhias is shattered by
the *dyskolos*.

The comedy of Sostratos' frustration is now augmented by a
new figure, Knemon's daughter herself, whose entry introduces
the second essential situation, the lost pot. Like Chaireas and
Pyrrhias, she is prominent in only a single scene, and like them
she is modelled after a recognizable type. This time, however,
the model is tragic. Her opening lament, her reference to Knemon's servant (Pan's 'old serving woman' and Pyrrhias'
'wretched old woman') as a nurse, and perhaps her gestures
and very appearance with a water jar are calculated tragic
echoes.[9] Her appeal to the nymphs, which reflects the piety Pan
had attributed to her, confirms the seriousness of her character,
as do her concern for the old woman's safety and her reluctance
to disturb the sacrificers at Pan's shrine. Her appearance introduces the first hint of a serious mode, and it is linked to the one
situation that will have a serious effect upon Knemon. Yet the
hint is gentle and works in counterpoint with Sostratos' comic

asides. As in the opening scene of the *Aspis*, Menander juxtaposes a tragically posed character and a comic one. Both scenes
are essentially expository – the one full of background information, the other explaining the lost pot – and both use the
contrast between the two figures to reveal something about the
comic one. Sostratos is again momentarily dumbfounded.
When faced with the girl's evident distress he can only articulate a string of oaths and an expression of amazement until he
collects his wits sufficiently to address her (191ff.).[10] His success at helping the girl restores his sagging spirits, however, and
he eventually leaves the stage confident that all will turn out
well. His self-apostrophe, like his earlier response to Chaireas
and Pyrrhias, reflects an ability to see himself objectively that
makes Sostratos, though perhaps a weak character, nevertheless a likeable one.

This succession of events has introduced two situations, the
young man in love and the lost pot, but it makes no connection
between them. Instead, it focuses attention on two characters:
Sostratos, around whom the action seems to revolve, and
Knemon, toward whom it looks. Chaireas and Pyrrhias fled at
his approach, Sostratos is intimidated by him, and the girl
leaves abruptly because she thinks he is coming out. It is,
however, Daos who enters, another minor figure used to introduce another ingredient, the tension between city and country.
Daos' appearance now, only some twenty-five lines before the
end of the act, both rounds off the action presented so far and
looks ahead to the next development.[11] His is the first articu-
lated country view, and it is one of bitterness and automatic
suspicion (208ff.). His comments on the scene between Sostratos and the girl introduce the theme of the next act, but by
keeping Daos apart Menander holds that theme in reserve. In
his final monologue Daos gives still another view of Knemon
which concludes the expository portrait that has been the
theme of this act. Daos is the first character to comment seriously on Knemon's way of life by suggesting the harm it can do.
Whereas Pan had treated him as a comic type and Pyrrhias'
description was tinged with farce, Daos' bitter attack points to
the darker side of misanthropy that will provide the turning
point of the action. The contrast between his view and the

preceding ones is a strategically placed reminder that Knemon
is ungeneralizable and will prove to be a type apart.

The countryman's distrust of Sostratos and his motives is
soon developed in Act II as Knemon's estranged step-son
Gorgias taxes Daos for not having taken stronger measures.
Gorgias is determined to intervene to protect his half-sister,
and the suggestion that they approach Knemon themselves
brings a spontaneous expression of terror from Daos. Fear of
Knemon again looms large, but the necessity is removed by the
return of Sostratos. Having failed to find Getas, Sostratos
returns alone, resolved to approach Knemon directly. His
explanation for Getas' absence introduces the final situation of
the play, his mother's sacrifice to Pan, which Sostratos treats
with characteristic casualness. His own situation is his prime
concern, and he is once again to be frustrated. Though determined to confront Knemon, the best he achieves is a confrontation with Gorgias (269ff.) This confrontation again reflects well
on Sostratos.[12] Gorgias begins by making a speech that is
extremely formal and stilted. Only after thirteen lines of
moralizing does he address Sostratos directly with a second
person verb, and even then his charge is indirect (284).
Whereas Gorgias tries hard to be general, Sostratos is at once
explicit and personal. He forces Gorgias to come to the point by
putting the essence of his entire speech into a single sentence:
'Do you think I've done something unseemly?' (288). Gorgias
must say what he means, but he still clings to the formality of
parallel participles and expands the alleged wrong-doing into a
pompous 'deed worthy of a thousand deaths' (289–93). Sostratos, who has done nothing at all improper, is clearly taken
aback, and he is carefully polite at trying to get a word in (293,
299–300). When he does get the chance, his reply is simple and
direct. His defence is the honesty of his intentions, reinforced by
his natural candour and modesty, and it has the desired effect
upon Gorgias. The young farmer becomes more conciliatory,
and Sostratos, always quick to recognize a helper, realizes that
he can be useful.

Gorgias' first bit of help takes the form of still another
description of Knemon and the difficulty of approaching him
(323ff.). This description is an amplification of Pan's original

portrait and uses familiar elements of the stock characterization; though Gorgias has finally cut the length of his sentences,
his structures remain formal.[13] But Gorgias also adds the hint
of another side to Knemon's nature, his appreciation of honest
work and his distrust of leisure. Gorgias sees a chance to
approach him through this positive trait, and Sostratos is anxious to go along. Now Daos puts in a word, and at his suggestion
Sostratos agrees to work beside them in the field. The ever-
suspicious Daos has been held in reserve until this point, where
his maliciously intended proposal caps the plan. It will, of
course, come to nothing since they will not find Knemon in the
field, but Sostratos' willingness to shoulder a mattock will
increase Gorgias' respect for him and will furnish the material
for a later, brilliant monologue. With this decision Sostratos
again reverts to type. He avoids a direct appeal to Knemon and
once again relies on the advice of others.

The scene is written with great skill. The contrast in style
between Sostratos and Gorgias economically distinguishes
them while the misunderstanding with which the meeting
begins and the abrupt reversal that ends it ensure a comic
undercurrent to maintain interest and amusement. But despite
the care in construction, the characters themselves seem
limited and ultimately uninteresting. Daos is a utilitarian figure enlivened only by his sullenness, and he disappears as a
speaking character after line 378. Gorgias' attitudes are stiff
and predictable. Sostratos is weak and equally predictable. He
is motivated more by the necessities of dramatic romance than
by an individualised passion, and his constant reliance on
others strongly implies that his fate will not be determined by
his own actions. Pan's prologue has promised as much, and it is
noteworthy that Pan phrased his intervention as the result of
interest in the *girl*, not in Sostratos. His limitations as a central
character lie at the heart of the discomfort with which early
critics discussed the play; when the *Dyskolos* is summarised as
the story of Sostratos' romance it does not sound very interesting.[14] The key ingredient lacking from Sostratos' character is
the ability to articulate his emotions. He tells Chaireas he is
lovesick and he admits as much to Gorgias, but his only expansion of this theme is a factual explanation of the action he has

taken. By leaving the lover's feelings unexpressed Menander eliminates the opportunity for psychological tensions that might advance him beyond his type and impress the audience too deeply. The self-irony that increases our liking for him also keeps him at a distance. Gorgias, too, is kept at a distance. His function in the play is not unlike Habrotonon's in the *Epitrepontes*. The independent threads of the action are connected through his intervention, and as a farmer he keeps the rustic perspective before us in Knemon's absence. But he is not granted the lively mind and complex motivation that individualised Habrotonon, nor does he occasionally seize the limelight. His attitudes are never a surprise; when he takes charge his heroism is enacted off-stage, and Sostratos tells of it. Menander deliberately flattens the characterization of his two young men to prevent them from overshadowing the *dyskolos*. Their confrontation is neatly divided between bringing them together in Sostratos' interest and discussing the difficulties of approaching Knemon. Once again other characters look toward Knemon.

With Sostratos' affairs well in hand, Menander now reintroduces the broad comedy he had suspended after Pyrrhias' exit in Act I. A cook enters with a sheep, soon followed by a slave staggering under a heavy load. Both are familiar comic figures, and they reinforce their comic appearance with equally familiar lines, the cook with stock jokes on making mincemeat and the slave with an exaggerated complaint (398ff.). This slave is immediately identified as Getas, whom Sostratos had linked with his mother's intention to sacrifice. Getas has hired the cook for this purpose and proceeds to explain the circumstances that led to the sacrifice: Sostratos' mother had a dream in which Pan put fetters on her son, dressed him in work clothes, and gave him a mattock (412ff.). As an obvious echo of the action planned for Sostratos, the dream connects the sacrifice motif with the young man's romance. It also puts further distance between the audience and Sostratos by the reminder that Sostratos' destiny is out of his hands. Equally significant is the fact that Menander constructs this link with wholly comic characters. By linking the gentle irony of Sostratos' romance with the broad comedy of these two, Menander associates his

situation with gaiety and farce. Then, having linked the sacrifice and Sostratos, he links it with Knemon.

The *dyskolos* himself opens Act III, only to be confronted with
the arriving party. Sight of this new crowd brings further proof
of Knemon's misanthropy and a decision to stay at home rather
than risk contact with them outside.[15] Knemon's refusal to go
out is necessary to frustrate Gorgias' plan to meet him in the
field and to keep him where he can go after the lost pot himself.
Menander also embellishes his situation for comic effect. The
sacrificers are short of a cauldron, and the only way to get one is
to approach the *dyskolos*. Getas, like Pyrrhias before him, is
defeated by Knemon's ferocity and refusal to become involved.
Though Getas is no coward and can return tit for tat in a comic
exchange, his mission is unsuccessful, and he leaves the field to
Knemon (468ff.). Next comes the cook, who claims a special
expertise in making such requests. His monologue explaining
the technique he will use, though noteworthy for its liveliness
and its role in setting up the next bit of farce, is a stock device
not of cooks, but of parasites. As he says, 'a man needing
something has to be ingratiating' (492–3). Though the
assembling of his equipment is a standard opportunity for a
cook's speech, Menander does not develop the motif in the
familiar way. Rather than let the cook develop his own theme,
Menander harnesses his potential for practical ends.[16] The
comic expansion of the request is done by Knemon, and the
cook must admit to being thoroughly beaten.

> I've come to ask for a stewing pot. :: I haven't got
> a stewing pot nor an axe nor salt nor
> vinegar nor anything else, but I have told everyone
> in the neighbourhood plainly, don't come near me.
> . . . . . .
>   Thanks a lot. :: I don't want
> any thanks from you people. :: Well then, no thanks. ::
> What incurable troubles! :: He's given me a real
> pounding.   (505–15)

This inability of the broad characters Pyrrhias, Getas, and
Sikon the cook to get the better of Knemon puts him in a unique
position. Menander is using the figure of the misanthrope for

comic effect, but by compressing and rationing out these farcical approaches he prevents his *dyskolos* from being identified as
a completely farcical character himself.

The differing descriptions of him also work against a simple
identification, and the situation that affects him most profoundly is carefully kept distinct from farce. Whereas Sostratos'
romance is linked to the broad comedy of the sacrificers, the lost
pot was introduced by Knemon's daughter with tragic overtones. Now in Act III, as the situation at the well becomes more
complex, Menander again chooses a tragic model for representing it. The old serving woman Simiche enters as a tragic
exangelos to announce grave news within. Like the nurse in
Euripides' *Hippolytos*, she reports the misfortune that triggers
the play's climax, and she too is followed on-stage by the
principal character. Simiche, however, is deprived of a sympathetic audience and abruptly breaks off her account at the
sound of the opening door. Yet despite Getas' uncharitable
comments about her, he is sufficiently moved by her dilemma
to offer help, and even after Knemon's abusive reply to her,
Getas closes the scene with an expression of sympathy. His
reference to battling against the rocks echoes the prologue and
puts a better construction on Knemon's lot than the complaint
with which Daos closed Act I. The serious mode first suggested
by modelling the girl and nurse on tragic types begins to surface
as Getas' rudeness and initial lack of sympathy are momentarily subdued by the problem they face.

Act IV begins with a seeming repeat of this scene, but this
time it is played before a different audience. Simiche is again
the tragic *exangelos* with the final news that Knemon himself has
fallen into the well, but Sikon refuses to be anything other than
the comic cook. He reverses the tragic expectation by receiving
the news with unabashed glee and the suggestion that Simiche
fix the old man permanently (629ff.). Only the timely appearance of Sostratos and Gorgias saves the day. This scene is the
closest Menander comes to representing the cook along conventional lines, and it is the last bit of broad humour until the
finale. Sikon's language is coloured by frequent oaths, each to a
different divinity, and the literal turn of a proverb. He is
inquisitive and verbose, and the moral he draws from the

mishap – that one should never wrong a cook – is a common manifestation of a *mageiros'* self-importance. His malicious glee capitalises on the comic wish to punish the misanthrope, but his contrast with the other characters awakens a more sympathetic undercurrent. Simiche's only thought, despite her harsh treatment, was to save Knemon. Gorgias and Sostratos run to the rescue, and Sikon himself reports the daughter's cry of anguish within the house. By leaving the stage to Sikon alone, Menander isolates his vengeful attitude from those closest to Knemon. Thus even in the finale, which Sikon's taunts in some sense prefigure, Simiche is kept apart from the developing farce. She will be unaffected by Getas' sharpness of tongue and by the change of metre, and she will not be part of the stage action taking shape. Comic opposition to the *dyskolos* is beginning to settle on the coarse, stock figures only, leaving space for sympathy and some degree of reconciliation between Knemon and the more individualised characters Sostratos and Gorgias.

The humanisation of Sostratos began with his work in the field. Though Menander chose to keep Sostratos' mental state in shadow to prevent too deep an identification with him, he is more willing to portray Sostratos' physical state in detail because of its comic potential. Sostratos' monologue describing his experience with the mattock capitalises on his capacity for wry self-description and his essential innocence (522ff.). The progress of pain up his back is told in graphic detail calculated to elicit a superior laugh from experienced workmen and amused sympathy from the more urbane. Yet he still relies on Gorgias, and the mysterious power of Pan's shrine to attract him reminds us of the greater forces at work upon him. Our superior knowledge continues to keep Sostratos at a distance, but his highly individual narrative style, enlivened by its humour and the use of *oratio recta* in reporting Gorgias' role, accentuates his likeable traits and begins to develop a kind of sympathy for him. This process of increased sympathy is continued with his next monologue, which describes the rescue of Knemon from the well (666ff.). Once again Gorgias was in charge and actually ran the risk of descending after the old man while Sostratos stood by with one hand on the rope and both eyes on the girl, but it is Sostratos' excited description of his own hapless lovesickness that attracts attention. His initial exclamations also divert attention from Sikon and the coarse humour he represents. In place of the broad jibes and self-importance with which Sikon greeted the news, Sostratos' narrative introduces the more subtle humour of his innocent inflation of these events to cosmic proportions and the confessed modesty of his own role in them. Though for Sostratos too Knemon's accident was timely, it is the rescue (and the opportunity to be near the girl) that cheers him. Sostratos' inability to play the hero's part himself is countered by his ability to describe the girl as if a goddess and by turning Gorgias into a Titan. He again wins sympathy by the openness of his description and the infectious joy with which he narrates it. He is even about to take us into his confidence, but once again his plans are disrupted by the *dyskolos* as the old man himself is suddenly wheeled on-stage (689ff.).

The serious mode used to colour the development of Knemon's situation all along reaches a height with this appearance on the *ekkyklema*. He enters like a stricken hero of tragedy, a stance carefully foreshadowed by having modelled the narration of his mishap on a tragic pattern. In Euripides' *Herakles*, for example, the catastrophe of the hero's madness is announced by Iris and Lyssa. A chorus, punctuated by cries from within, builds suspense, and then a messenger enters to report how the mad Herakles has killed his wife and small children. Only then do the hero and his murdered family appear. This is the structure Menander adapts for the *Dysokolos*.[17] Simiche's call for help pre-figures the action, while Sikon's monologue performs the function of a chorus. It, too, is punctuated by an off-stage cry, and dramatization of his expectations whets our own. Sostratos is the messenger. In place of having a chorus to address he speaks directly to the audience. Then he gives details of the rescue and prepares for the entrance of the hero himself; his tendency to inflate the magnitude of these events is perhaps an unconscious echo of the tragic function he fulfils. As in the opening scene of the *Aspis* and the arbitration scene of the *Epitrepontes*, Menander uses the tragic pattern not for parody but to guide his audience's expectations and colour its perceptions. Though he does not forego comedy entirely, the thrust of this scene is in another direction. The treatment of Knemon has hinted at a serious underside, and now the explicit association prepares us to see something of it.

As sometimes happens in tragedy, the metre changes to trochaic tetrameters to mark a passage that climaxes development of the plot.[18] Like Euripides' Iphigenia at Aulis, Knemon cuts the dramatic knot by renouncing the position that has obstructed progress of the inevitable action (708ff.). In explaining and amending his character, his speech integrates the variant perspectives presented by others. The description of his own conduct parallels those given by Pan and Gorgias (724–6, cf. 9–10, 332–5). His discovery of responsibility toward other people answers Daos' earlier complaint about his treatment of his daughter (715–17, cf. 222–4), and Knemon accepts for himself the adjectives 'harsh and grouchy' ($\chi\alpha\lambda\epsilon\pi\delta\varsigma$ $\delta\acute{v}\sigma\kappa\omega\lambda\delta\varsigma$ $\tau\varepsilon$, 747, cf. 242, 325). His excuse is the world's selfishness and dishonesty, which echoes his complaint in Act III about the greed and hypocrisy of sacrificers, but Gorgias' deed has taught Knemon the limitations of this view. He therefore proposes the changes that make possible the play's happy resolution, but they have a curious limitation of their own. Knemon's acknowledgement of social responsibility is immediately followed by his delegation of it. He explicitly wishes to continue living his own way, and his reason for adopting Gorgias is to avoid the social intercourse otherwise necessary to secure his daughter's future. When Gorgias attempts to bring Sostratos forward, Knemon will not wish to become involved. The poignancy of his speech lies in this evident price for his misanthropy. He is wet and shaken, and he relies on his daughter for physical support. He must confess his error, but he cannot change his ways. Like Molière's Alceste he spurns the sympathy offered him, and like Shakespeare's Timon he is prepared to die as he lived, alone. His monologue, so solemn in form and sentiment, concludes the chain of situations that have been presented with consistent tragic overtones. The fall down the well which motivates it links the lost pot and the scattered descriptions of Knemon's character into the dramatic *praxis* that profoundly affects his relatives and his household.

The link between this action and the romance surrounding

Sostratos still remains to be made, but Menander has prepared for it by a mixture of modes. We know that Knemon will not really die, and his serious confession is juxtaposed with Sostratos' lighter situation. The young lover has been kept in the background, but he remains present as a comic figure. Knemon snarled at his love-lorn sigh when the girl puts her arms around the old man and his only other acknowledgement of Sostratos, mention of the sunburn, recalls the lover's most comic moment. Gorgias also recalls this moment and links it to the betrothal he is now empowered to make. Sostratos' presence, like Smikrines' at the beginning of the *Aspis* and like Moschion's during the recognition scene of the *Perikeiromene*, prevents the tragic colouring from becoming too strong by preparing for the comic developments that follow. With the *dyskolos* wheeled back in, Gorgias' comic attempt at a betrothal reasserts a light mode (761ff.). He juxtaposes the verbs for betrothing the girl and granting a dowry in some haste to fit the formal words in, and he concludes with a characteristically convoluted bit of moralizing about the reward of virtue.[19] They are interrupted, however, by the arrival of Sostratos' father Kallipides, whose only thought is for his delayed meal. His mention of the sheep recalls the antics of the cook who brought it and the noisy crowd of sacrificers. The act that began with a tragic *exangelos* thus ends with an echo of past comedy and the promise of a happy resolution to come.

The marriage of Gorgias to Sostratos' sister is the first element of this resolution. Gorgias has consistently served a double function, and he now receives the second portion of a double reward.[20] As an industrious farmer he represented the better side of Knemon's nature, and he defended the interests of Knemon's household. For this he was rewarded by being made Knemon's heir. Gorgias also linked the misanthrope's situation with the love interest by being Sostratos' sympathetic advisor, and he now receives the reward for this loyalty. It is arranged by Sostratos in a sudden reversal of their respective roles. Sostratos proposes the marriage and forces his father to agree (797ff.). The argument he uses – the need for employing wealth wisely – is a philosophic commonplace. What is striking is that it comes from him. Gorgias has been the moralizer. Pan introduced him with a gnomic phrase, and he first confronted Sostratos with a series of moral pronouncements. Sostratos then forced him to come to the point with the suppressed impatience of the young sophisticate. Maxims, as Aristotle noted in his work on rhetoric, are the perogative of the elderly and the experienced, but they are a sign of rusticity and boorishness in the young. Yet now Sostratos himself adopts this mannerism, and it is Kallipides who grows impatient. He is tired of moralising and urges Sostratos to go off and arrange things. Sostratos' ability to win his father to the marriage, followed by Gorgias' eventual acceptance of the arrangement, resolves the tension between city and country and between rich and poor that has surfaced at intervals through the play. The contact Sostratos has had with both sides enables him to bridge the differences. The experience in Phyle has not left him unchanged. In his last appearance Sostratos seems to grow in dramatic presence, but his newly-won maturity is soon undercut by an innocent boast. Once again he resorts to a maxim ('everything is attainable by diligence and hard work', 862), and he offers himself as an example because he has achieved a marriage no man thought possible. This is partly true, of course, but he did not get the girl without considerable help from Gorgias and not without the connivance of Pan. The resulting irony of Sostratos' self-congratulation preserves his comic image. Unlike Charisios of the *Epitrepontes* and, as well shall see, unlike Moschion of the *Samia*, the conclusion does not bring Sostratos the self-knowledge that will foster true sympathy for him. He still understands less about his affairs than we do, and that extra knowledge continues the distance between him and us.

The second element of the resolution involves Knemon, whose presence hovers just behind the scene. The moral argument Sostratos uses with his father has distinct echoes of Knemon's own situation. The observation that position brings responsibility is precisely the lesson Knemon has had to learn, and some might hear in the statement that an open friend is more valuable than hidden wealth an allusion to Timon and his buried hoard. Nor has Knemon's *dyskolia*, though tempered by his mishap, been entirely supplanted. Both Sostratos and Gorgias wish to include him in the festivities, but he persistently refuses (852ff., 867ff.). Simiche's warning that no good will come of his recalcitrance echoes Daos' earlier foreboding and suggests that further trouble lies ahead for him (875–8, cf. 220–6). Knemon's final appearance is in a musical fantasia based upon these hints and the comic approach to the *dyskolos* that has unified so much of the preceding action.

A pipe his heard, and the metre changes to iambic tetrameters. Getas' remark to the piper calls attention to the change and deliberately makes us aware of the dramatic illusion (880). Just as Pan had introduced the artificial scene by telling us to imagine Phyle, Getas now signals the approaching finale by a similar reminder. His appearance with Sikon re-introduces the broad humour they have consistently represented, and the revenge they plan on Knemon is a further development of their comedy in Act III. That earlier humour had developed gradually. Getas' request for a cauldron was natural enough in its context. Sikon's involvement, enlivened by his set speech on techniques for borrowing, and the spectacle of Knemon's increasing rage broaden the comedy. Their escalated demands now, without any real context, move the motif fully into the realm of farce. With Knemon carried outside first Sikon, then Getas, and then the two together torment him with outrageous requests (912ff.). One small cauldron becomes any number of large cauldrons and is quickly followed by requests for bowls, tables, carpets, and a bronze mixing bowl, all rather grand objects neither the pair is likely to need nor Knemon at all likely to have on hand. The resulting structural link with the earlier action is strengthened by a thematic link, for this ragging is the final price Knemon must pay for his misanthropy. By sending everyone away he has left himself undefended, and he is reduced to the same misery (*dystychia*) to which he had previously reduced others (919, cf. 574). Sikon taunts him with this fact in the last description Knemon receives (931ff.). Coming just after the old man's threat to 'kill that Simiche', Sikon's remark that he avoids crowds, hates women, and refuses to have anything to do with sacrificers sounds much like the *dyskolos* of old. The traditional vocabulary of misanthropy appears once again. This time, however, owing largely to Sikon's long-restrained loquacity and Knemon's weakened

constitution, the approachers overwhelm him. The old man is
almost literally swept away by their energy and carried to the
celebration in spite of himself. The play Pan began with an
appeal to imagination and the description of a traditional
comic misanthrope ends with a fantastic triumph over the same
figure. What has come between is a romance designed to
dramatise the various facets of his misanthropy and provide
elements for a victory over it.

Menander's dexterity in weaving the diverse threads of his
play into a unified fabric is considerable. The decision to
develop Knemon's character indirectly enabled him to reveal
its comic side through Pyrrhias, Getas, and Sikon and its
serious side through the tragically posed daughter and servant
and the virtuous industry of Gorgias. Sostratos' hunting trip to
Phyle was the catalyst for bringing these elements together, and
through his happiness happiness comes to others. The *Dyskolos*
is thus pre-eminently a play of combined modes and situations
united around the traditional figure of the misanthrope. It is an
extremely skillful play, but not an entirely satisfying one, for it
lacks inner tension. The great power Menander's plays can
generate comes from representation of the inner conflicts their
situations can produce: the agony of Polemon in the
Perikeiromene learning the consequences of his rash act,
Charisios' sudden realisation of his own hypocrisy in the *Epitrepontes*. This kind of power is missing from the *Dyskolos*. The
dark side of misanthropy is developed as something detached
from Knemon. Like Polemon and Charisios he suffers in a
situation of his own making, but his suffering is not represented
in personal terms. Though for a moment he reveals his inner
torment, he relieves the crisis by the mechanical expedient of
adopting Gorgias, and his final reconciliation is set as a deliberate fantasy. The countryman's distrust of city folk is naïvely
removed by Sostratos' willingness to shoulder a mattock in his
own interest, and the antagonism of rich and poor is swept
away in Kallipides' formulaic indulgence of his son. Though
the events of the play alter the circumstances of all its characters, the changes are largely external. Menander eliminates
difficulties without really resolving them. In the *Dyskolos* he
reveals his skill in structuring events, but not yet his ability to

develop personalities. For this demonstration we must examine a play in which the combination of modes and situations is designed both to weave a plot and to reveal the frailties and strengths of its characters not only to the audience, but to themselves.

VII

Sania (The Samian Woman): A Play of Successful Combinations

Like most Menandrean prologues, the speech with which young Moschion opens the *Samia* introduces the central characters, provides necessary background information, and indicates the direction of the action to come. It functions much like Pan's prologue to the *Dyskolos* or the speeches by Misapprehension and Fortune in the *Perikeiromene* and *Aspis*, except for one significant detail. Menander generally uses a divine prologue speaker to colour our perceptions of his characters and situations and to shape our expectations, often by including a piece of information human characters do not know: Glykera was actually embracing her brother, Kleostratos is alive, Sostratos' love has been engineered by a god. Divinities who speak prologues emphasize the distance between audience and actors by sharing their omniscience and by reminding us that the figures on stage are subject to their greater power. There is no suggestion of a greater power in the *Samia* and no distance fostered between audience and actors. The figures of this play are all too responsible for their own actions, and our perceptions are coloured not so much by our omniscience as by our frustration at the sight of good intentions continually hampered by weakness of character. Moschion's marriage to the girl next door, a universally desired union, is jeopardised by his reluctance to admit an embarrassing truth. Moschion's father Demeas suddenly disrupts his own relationship with the Samian woman Chrysis because of hasty, ill-founded suspicions. The action combines the obstructed marriage found in the *Dyskolos* with the disrupted union of the *Perikeiromene* and *Misoumenos*. The sequence of misunderstandings that weaves the two situations into a plot develops not so much from lack of knowledge as from the fear to use it.[1] The action of the *Samia* is preeminently a product of character, and the need for special care in character-isation leads Menander to abandon the divine prologue and open his play with an expository speech by Moschion himself.

Strepsiades' complaint about his son at the beginning of Aristophanes' *Clouds* reminds us that the relationship between father and son – the main theme of Moschion's narrative – is a common motif in Greek comedy.[2] Having married the niece of an aristocrat, a 'Megakles' Megakles', the plain and hard-working Strepsiades has produced a son of extravagant, sophisticated tastes. Strepsiades must now deal with the resulting debts, and his resentment and desire to avoid payment eventually lead him to Socrates' Reflectory. In *The Wasps* Aristophanes builds a different set of actions around a similar dilemma by reversing roles; the son cannot control the father. The old man Philokleon, like the young Plautine lovers Strabax in the *Truculentus* and Philolaches in the *Mostellaria*, must woo a flute girl with promises contingent upon the death of his son, who is a harsh cress-shavingcuminsplitter. As in *The Clouds*, the dramatic action develops out of the conflict between generations. For the *Samia* Menander inverts the dilemma and refashions the expository device of *The Clouds*. Like Strepsiades' wife and son, Moschion has been raised in luxury, but it is with his father's encouragement. Demeas adopted Moschion as a child and gave him every advantage. Whereas Strepsiades complained about sophisticated living, Moschion's prologue glows with the vocabulary of urbane virtues. He prides himself on his sophistication. He has been cheerfully granted horses and dogs, and he has learned to be generous in his turn. The possessor of all these virtues and advantages has nevertheless got himself into a terrible fix, and his explanation shows far better then he realizes both how he got into it and why he will be unable to extricate himself unaided.[3]

While Demeas was away Moschion got the neighbour's daughter pregnant and promised to marry her. The girl bore a child, which Chrysis is now raising as her own, and he awaits his father's return with understandable anxiety. But Moschion cannot state matters so baldly. He is suffering keenly from a shame and embarrassment that colour his entire narrative. He delays telling the crucial facts, first by describing Demeas' character, and then by describing the festive circumstances under which the rape took place. He uses the story of the festival to work up to the main point, which he then hurries over as quickly as possible: 'The girl became pregnant. In telling this I also say what went before' (49–50). Then he buries the admission in an emphatic declaration of responsibility and of honourable intentions. The difficulty he foresees is in securing Demeas' agreement to the marriage, and to show why this is so, Moschion attempts to explain what Demeas is like. Moschion's real source of difficulty, however, is his inability to see beyond his own limited perspective, and this is what the description of Demeas actually demonstrates. He speaks of Demeas only in terms of himself. His verbs are almost entirely first person singulars; adjectives refer to himself. 'Through him', says Moschion, 'I was somebody' (17). He offers himself as the measure of what Demeas is, and in doing so he turns an analysis of the father into a portrait of the son. Nor, when speaking of Demeas' liaison with Chrysis, can he keep himself out of the picture. Foremost in Moschion's mind is the embarrassment of his own current predicament.

> I hesitate to tell the rest. Perhaps I'm ashamed.
> There's no help for it, yet I *am* ashamed.   (47–8)

This kind of embarrassment is fairly common among the indiscreet young men of comedy. 'I'm only afraid to face the father,' a lover tells his friend in an unidentified fragment of Menander (fr. 598 K–T, cf. *Fab. Inc.* 26). 'I won't be able to look him in the eye, since I've wronged him.' In ascribing a similar feeling to his father, however, Moschion is simply projecting his own sense of shame onto Demeas. Similarly, his condescension in explaining Demeas' attachment as 'a human enough occurrence' and his claim to have encouraged the liaison stamp the account with his own personality. That Demeas was reluctant to have his son involved is certainly credible, but we have only Moschion's testimony for the reason.[4]

This speech demonstrates three things about Moschion. First is his remarkable egotism. He tells us his story because *he* has the time, and he explains every character and action in terms of his own feelings and conduct. Second is his moral cowardice. He hesitates to speak of the rape and shrinks from telling his father. Even his protestations of honourable intentions is suspect because of its very earnestness, and indeed, his slave Parmenon must soon remind him quite bluntly of his obligations (67–9). Third is his foolishness. His attempt to avoid one charge will involve the innocent Chrysis in a second, more serious one. Moschion can neither see the implications of his acts, nor is he willing to take responsibility for them. By having him speak for himself, Menander enables these aspects of his personality to permeate the narrative. When divinities portray character their terse descriptions are subordinate to a greater design. The portrait of that other Moschion in the *Perikeiromene*, of Smikrines in the *Aspis*, and even Pan's description of Knemon are accorded due, but limited place in a sequential narrative. Though these figures may influence the play's direction, they will be overcome by events turning not exclusively on their personalities but on the emergence of an unsuspected truth or a sudden catastrophe. Moschion's loquaciousness here in the *Samia* and the lack of anything entirely unknown create a different set of priorities.

The personalities of the fathers Demeas and Nikeratos will also shape the action, and their first appearance delineates and distinguishes between them. They enter from the harbour with their baggage train, newly arrived from Pontos and very glad to be home (96ff.).[5] Demeas clearly commands. He instructs the porters and leads the conversation, changing topics from their safe arrival to the marriage between their children that they have previously discussed. His is the quick-witted, dominant personality, and Nikeratos looks to him for answers. Nikeratos himself is slower, and so more comic. He replies to Demeas first with a disjointed complaint about the food, drink, and people of Pontos that probably embodies stock jokes about the undesirability of the place.[6] When Demeas answers his question about the weather there facetiously, Nikeratos takes him literally, and he must make Demeas' indirect reference to the proposed marriage explicit. Nikeratos is the first character presented as overtly and entirely comic. We have seen how Menander uses such stock figures as a cook in the *Aspis* and *Dyskolos* to pace outbreaks of humour as the action requires. In the *Samia* this function will reside largely in Nikeratos. This initial scene, in which Demeas' control of the conversation provides opportunities for Nikeratos' comedy, has a kind of structural parallel at *Aspis* 216–49, where Daos controls the action but becomes a foil for the cook and caterer. The dominance of Demeas' personality is countered by the humour in Nikeratos', and in the action to come Menander will draw upon his comic potential to control the emotional temperature of Demeas' most dramatic moments.

Demeas influences events largely through the quick temper and tendency toward precipitous action that are his main weaknesses. Both faults surface at once in Act II as he responds to the news of Chrysis' 'child' with a very ill grace. He refers to her with sardonic irony as a 'married hetaira' (130) and, if the restoration is correct, calls the child 'secret' (132). Since Chrysis' social position and that of any children by her union with Demeas depend upon his attitude toward them, the repudiation implied by his language is particularly serious.[7] By calling the child clandestine, though he was certainly informed of it at the earliest possible moment, he presumably means that it was not conceived with his prior consent, an unreasonable but not unheard of attitude for a father to adopt. He wishes to put all the blame on Chrysis and to sever their relationship. At line 135 he refers to her in the masculine to emphasize her remoteness. Moschion meets this tirade first with feigned ignorance of its cause, and then with a studied glibness.

> For heaven's sake, who among us is legitimate
> and who a bastard? We're all born men. :: You're
> joking. :: Dionysos! I'm entirely serious.
> I don't think birth determines breeding. Good
> character is the test. The honest man is
> legitimate, and the wicked one a bastard.   (137–42)

The poignancy of these statements on legitimacy coming from an adopted son is gently undercut by our knowledge that Moschion has been off practising speeches (94–5). Though his mind drifted in other directions, fine phrases remain on the tip of his tongue. The papyrus is torn away at this point, but his arguments, whatever they were, must have been successful.

Demeas apparently agreed to keep Chrysis and the child in his house, and when the text resumes after a gap of some sixteen lines, Moschion is winning his agreement to his own quick marriage. These expository scenes concentrate not on action but on character drawing to make the rapid sequence of actions to come seem credible and perhaps even inevitable. Demeas' display of anger in Act II engenders no immediate action, but it prefigures the attitude and action one further piece of information will cause him to take toward Chrysis.

The pace quickens in Act III as we begin to see the influence character will have on action. Demeas has had a shock, which he explains in a monologue similar in length and impact to Moschion's introduction. Just as Moschion's prologue centred on his embarrassment, so Demeas' monologue hinges on a central image, a nurse fondling an infant. In the bustle of preparations for the wedding the child was momentarily left unattended, and Demeas has overheard Moschion's old nurse soothe it with 'the sort of things nurses say' (242). Unfortunately for his peace of mind, one of these things indicated that the child is Moschion's. This central vignette is depicted in considerable detail and perhaps gains impact from its visual associations. Precisely such images of an old woman with a baby on her lap are common among the terracotta figurines of this period.[8] As a structural unit in the monologue, it picks up the earlier mention of the child and looks ahead to Demeas' later, damning report that he has seen Chrysis herself nursing it. The monologue dramatises the growing impact of the discovery on Demeas. He begins with a solemn, ominous prologue to raise our expectations. A sudden storm at sea can turn a smooth voyage into a catastrophe, and this is what has happened to him. He then slips into domestic details. At the end of Act II we saw Demeas shouting instructions for the wedding preparations, and he now sketches the resulting turmoil (216ff.). We learn that the child was abandoned, that the nurse found it, and that she spoke indiscreetly. The impact of the news on Demeas is first indicated indirectly by his description of a second servant's alarm and haste to silence the nurse. Demeas himself struggles to maintain an outward calm. He wants to avoid hasty judgements, but he cannot really do so.

His immediate, cold reference to 'the Samian woman' (265) recalls his earlier attempt at detachment from her, and his haste to reassure himself about Moschion's character implies an intention to fix the blame elsewhere. His temper is barely under control, and precipitous action is again in the offing.

The monologue's skillful construction provides this lucid description of offstage action simultaneously with the insight into Demeas' present mental state. Several techniques contribute to its effectiveness. *Oratio recta* enlivens the account as Demeas imitates the shouts of slaves, the nurse's chatter, and the anxious dialogue between nurse and servant. Such opportunities for mimickry add needed colour to the eighty odd lines of narrative, just as the messenger's speech in the *Sikyonios*, which was perhaps a hundred, requires the actor to imitate the pleas of litigants and the shouts of a crowd. A second technique is the blending of static and dynamic portraits. The detailed description of the nurse, previously unmentioned and never again more than a *muta persona*, and the second servant's anxious whispers are striking, isolated images. *Oratio recta* gives them momentary, independent life, but they are soon submerged in the rising tide of Demeas' indignation. As the old man mulls over what he has heard his verbs become almost entirely first person (265–79). Like Moschion, he instinctively subordinates others to himself. A third device is the direct appeal to the audience, marked here by the interjected vocative 'gentlemen' (*andres*, 269). This type of address is common in comedy, but in the extant parts of the *Samia* only Demeas uses it consistently.[9] The informality of Moschion's opening speech created a certain rapport with the audience, and the immediacy of his prologue hinted at a special relationship to be developed with him. Menander, however, has played with the expectation. Demeas' frequent appeals to the audience establish that rapport with *him*, for the action is beginning to focus on Demeas.

Moschion left the stage at line 162 and will not appear again until Act IV. His concealment of the truth set the action in motion, and once he gained his father's approval of the marriage – a simple enough task since Demeas and Nikeratos both desired it – he can have little effect on the resulting complications. *Demeas'* discoveries and actions further the plot, and this monologue signals the increasing emphasis on his role. The familiar device of the overheard conversation both advances the action and alters its focus.[10] Its use here makes a significant contrast with Menander's dramatisation of the analogous situation at *Epitrepontes* 878–932. An overheard conversation is the basic ingredient there, too, but the structure is rather different. Charisios has overheard Smikrines and Pamphile discussing him. Onesimos first enters as an *exangelos* to explain what has happened and how his master has reacted. Then Charisios appears to reveal the depth of his distress and his determination to save his marriage. Both monologues make considerable use of direct speech, Onesimos' reported and Charisios' projected, and both are lively and dramatic. Yet by dividing the scene between Charisios and Onesimos, Menander has effectively reduced the young man's role. Attention moves from Onesimos to Charisios and will soon move again from Charisios to Habrotonon. Because the action of the *Epitrepontes* turns on surrogates, Charisios' appearance is integrated into theirs. In the *Samia* Menander combines the function of the *exangelos* and soliloquist in a single monologue. Demeas speaks entirely for himself, and by having him do so Menander puts him at the very centre of the action.

There is, of course, a certain comic irony in Demeas' situation as he claims certain knowledge of Chrysis' maternity, the one thing about which he is actually in error. Yet there is also the potential for considerable poignancy. Because the relationship between Demeas and Moschion is only by adoption, it must depend on trust and good will between them. The possibility that Moschion has betrayed him with Chrysis threatens the very basis of their relationship, and that is why Demeas is reluctant even to voice that possibility. The anguish of his position is genuine, and, as we know from Euripides' *Hippolytos*, it can be tragic. Menander is moving his play close to the border between serious and light, and we may wonder for a moment which way things will turn. The entrance of Parmenon with a cook, however, is an unmistakable signpost (283ff.).

The cook, as so often in Menander, immediately introduces the broad humour characteristic of his type. There are the

familiar jokes on making mincemeat, and his self-importance
threatens a tiresome loquacity as he strings five if-clauses
together in rapid succession. Parmenon answers in kind (*'if* you
haven't noticed', 293), and the two trade insults. There is also
the more subtle humour of Parmenon's blithe self-assurance on
the threshold of disaster as Demeas waits to be recognized. The
comedy of the following encounter is built from those weaknesses of Demeas' character that Act II revealed. He taxes Parmenon with the piece of truth he has just acquired without pausing
to listen to an explanation that might reveal the rest. He is also
violent, and his threats drive Parmenon off before he can speak.
This refusal to listen confirms Demeas in his error. He resolves
upon action, but whereas his earlier monologue was balanced
between serious and light, the speech in which he announces
his resolve is predominantly light (325ff.).

What makes this second monologue comic? It is certainly not
the content. As Demeas seeks to exonerate Moschion and save
their relationship his willingness to judge his son by past conduct without extending the same generosity to Chrysis is man-
ifestly unfair. He turns savagely on her, calling her 'my Helen'
(337) and 'whore, creature, plague' (348). He is about to throw
her out, and he announces his intention in a sentence marked
by biting sarcasm and harsh alliteration: ἐπὶ κεφαλὴν ἐς
κόρακας ὦσον τὴν καλήν/ Σαμίαν ('shove the handsome
Samian on her head to Hell', 353–4). Yet the style and context
undercut the seriousness of the content. Demeas begins with a
string of tragic-sounding exclamations, but he interrupts himself in midcourse:

> O city of Kekrops' land,
> O outspread aether, O – Demeas, why are you shouting?
>
> (325–6)

The effort to master his emotions leads him away from tragic
diction, and as he begins talking his manner becomes increasingly comic. His short, choppy sentences are characteristic of
comic figures in distress, and he again addresses the audience
directly. Sandwiched between these displays of emotion is the
torturous chain of logic that works him up to this agitated pitch.
He interprets Moschion's eagerness to marry as an attempt to

escape from Chrysis, who must have seduced him when drinking.

> I just can't believe that a boy
> so well-bred and moderate in everything
> to others would do such a thing to me,
> not if he were adopted ten times over and no
> son by birth. It's not his way. I know his character.
> The woman's a whore, a plague.   (343–8)

By making this chain explicit Menander enables us to identify
its errors. Demeas has misinterpreted both Chrysis' character
and Moschion's motive for wanting a quick marriage, and our
ability to pinpoint these mistakes begins to develop the distance
necessary for us to treat Demeas' anger as comedy. Context too
strengthens the comic tone. We cannot take as entirely serious
an old man who has just routed his slave with shouted threats.
He appeals to us to see the logic of his position, but because we
know both that his reasoning is faulty and that his farcical rage
has just eliminated an opportunity to correct it, we are more
aware of its comic lack of logic. The serious mode introduced by
the dilemmas of Moschion and Demeas and the light mode
represented by such characters as Nikeratos and the cook
are beginning to converge as Demeas' anger turns toward
action.

His expulsion of Chrysis is accompanied, as was his decision
to do it, by a certain cruelty and harshness of expression. He
bundles her unceremoniously out of the house with a few
possessions and the baby in her arms. To avoid mentioning
Moschion, Demeas can give her only an allusive explanation
and finally hides his lack of coherent excuse in a torrent of
abuse. It is a highly dramatic and potentially ugly scene. The
frankness of his monologue and our awareness of his error,
however, have created an amused sympathy for his predicament that is incompatible with harsh action. Menander therefore tempers the scene with a touch of comedy. The cook
returns just as Demeas is about to charge inside to rout Chrysis.
His glimpse of 'some crazy old man' puts the required comic
perspective on Demeas' behaviour while his aborted effort to
intervene softens the drama with farcical action (383ff.). Once

Demeas has slammed the door on Chrysis comedy resumes
with the appearance of Nikeratos, whose offer of refuge is
necessary for subsequent developments. Introducing the old
man with a sheep facilitates the transition from the cook's
comedy to Nikeratos', for complaints about an animal are a
motif common to cook's speeches (399ff., cf. *Dys.* 393ff.). Like
the cook, Nikeratos also passes judgement on the madness of
Demeas' behaviour, and the silliness of his explanation – the
unfavourable climate of Pontos has affected him – recalls
the humour of their arrival and ends the act on a note of
simple-minded charity. He is again the foil to Demeas, who
is acquiring attributes of the angry old man familiar in
comedy.

Act IV opens with the characters in these same apparent
roles. Nikeratos remains simple and benign as he announces his
intention to remonstrate with Demeas. Moschion, who has
spent his day at the baths waiting for sundown, is as self-
centred as ever. He does not return Nikeratos' friendly greeting, but voices his impatience in a continuation of his private
thoughts (428–33). When Demeas joins them on-stage he is still
angry and abusive. He again addresses the audience directly,
and frequent asides will signal his growing confusion. Convinced that he knows 'everything', Demeas will become
increasingly exasperated by Moschion's defence of Chrysis.
Moschion does not seem to appreciate the sacrifices he has
made to save their relationship, and Demeas' outrage at the
young man's apparent shamelessness makes him abusive and
willful as he finally challenges Moschion to admit the 'truth' to
Nikeratos. The seriousness of Demeas' anguish is eclipsed by
the comic irony of his misapprehension and the predicament
into which he has unwittingly thrust his son. Only Nikeratos'
slowness of wit saves the young man. Nikeratos has finally
grasped the essence of Demeas' suspicion, and the combination
of his over-stated denunciation and Moschion's bewilderment
at what he can possibly have in common with such sinners as
Tereus, Oedipus, Thyestes, and Phoenix turns the scene
toward farce (495ff.). Nikeratos' speech is a jumble of the
highflown and the mundane. *He*, he says, would immediately
sell such a mistress and disinherit such a son,

> . . . so that no barbershop is empty,
> no, nor stoa, but everyone will sit around from dawn
> chattering of me, saying what a man Nikeratos
> has become, who rightly prosecutes a murder.   (510–13)

Nikeratos consistently sprinkles his speech with the language of high poetry. He shows a tendency to call his bed a fourposter ($\lambda\acute{\epsilon}\kappa\tau\rho o\nu$, 507) and his house his hall ($\mu\acute{\epsilon}\lambda\alpha\theta\rho\alpha$, 517). Here he attaches a tragic set of negatives to the mundane image of gossipers in barbershop and stoa, and the colloquial 'chatters' contrasts with the overblown 'murder' to describe the subject of their talk. Equally significant is Nikeratos' desire to be thought 'a man', for this was also Demeas' thought as he steeled himself to expel Chrysis (349). Nikeratos' indignation parodies Demeas' earlier indignation, and he will soon re-enact the earlier drama as farce.

With Nikeratos safely inside, Moschion at last tells his father the truth, but only to avoid the more serious charge (526ff.) He is as reluctant as ever to face his responsibility, and when Nikeratos returns evidently upset, Moschion scurries away. Sight of the baby being nursed has again caused a crisis as the outraged bystander suddenly discovers he is the true victim. Nikeratos has seen his daughter with the infant. The news confirms the truth of Moschion's confession but raises a new set of difficulties. Having recognised and repented over his error, Demeas now reverts to his quick-witted, reasonable self; Nikeratos becomes the madman. He is beside himself with rage, and once thwarted in an attempt to destroy the evidence by burning out his family, he reverts to the idea of expelling Chrysis. Whereas Demeas' expulsion of Chrysis was saved from complete seriousness only by the presence of the cook and Nikeratos' timely arrival, this second expulsion is farcical from the beginning. Nikeratos races to and from his house in agitated confusion. There are sounds of pandemonium within, and the scene will end in slapstick with the two old men coming to blows as Demeas protects the woman and child (574ff.). Secure in his newly acquired knowledge of the true situation, Demeas holds himself aloof from events as he comments on Nikeratos' character and actions (548–56, 563–7). Menander uses the rapport established with Demeas to heighten the comedy by contrasting his calm with Nikeratos' excitement. This calm eventually prevails as Nikeratos abandons his plan to burn the baby and murder his wife. Demeas exerts the same control over him that he demonstrated in the first act, making Nikeratos walk off his anger and turning his extravagant language against him with the argument that the child was fathered by Zeus, though Moschion will certainly marry the girl.

By reversing the roles of Act III Menander moves the play towards broad comedy. A change of metre signals this alteration in tone at the outset as the increased length and regularity of the trochaic tetrameter quickens the tempo. Nikeratos' simplicity makes him a far more comic angry old man than Demeas, and the contrast between his constant motion and Demeas' stationary calm heightens the effect. The pace of the action itself increases as the web of misunderstanding woven over the previous three acts unravels in a single act with the truth brought home to both fathers. This linear progression is attended, as in the *Dyskolos* finale, by an internal parallelism. Menander builds this rapid, farcical act out of the comic potential present from the beginning in Nikeratos' character and from elements of the earlier drama repeated with the opposite mode dominant. Sight of the child being nursed is again the catalyst, but this time announced by Nikeratos' hysterical shouts. Chrysis is again expelled, but this time by a foolish rather than anguished old man. Demeas calms his neighbour with an explanation of events as deft and facetious as his earlier explanation of the weather in Pontos, and the act ends with the two of them reaching the same accord they had reached in their first appearance. The emergence of the truth, attended by a progression from Demeas' anguish to Nikeratos' farce, returns us to the equilibrium with which the play began.

This combination of progression and parallelism to weave elements of the play together appears again in the finale as the dramatic focus returns to Moschion. His scheme to punish his father by feigning to enlist in military service abroad is a further manifestation of his characteristic egotism. He refuses to admit to himself that Demeas' momentary injustice to him was a natural consequence of his own irresponsible desire to hide the truth. Moschion affects indignation to avoid this admission, and the resulting speech, for all its tragic overtones, has a hollow ring.[11] Despite his claim to be almost beside himself with emotion, he can still balance long clauses, and whereas Demeas' claim of indignation had steeled him to do something 'manly', Moschion expressly eliminates that possibility (630–1, cf. 349–50). All he really seeks is to shift the blame from himself, a desire Parmenon promptly articulates in a parallel monologue of his own (641–57). Parmenon's initial oath echoes Moschion's solemnity, but he goes on to disavow responsibility in the short sentences and self-address of comedy. His quick summary of the preceding action voices Moschion's implicit desire, and it echoes Demeas' earlier effort to excuse his son.

> My young master attacked a free-born
> girl. Parmenon certainly did nothing wrong.
> She got pregnant. Parmenon's not responsible.
> The little baby came into our own
> house. *He* brought it in, not I.
> Someone inside confessed the birth.
> What wrong did Parmenon do there?
> None.   (646–53, cf. 328, 537)

The absurdity of Moschion's plan is brought home by Parmenon's ignorance and the resulting slapstick, by Moschion's own doubts, and by his sudden fear that nobody will prevent his going. Its foolishness is underscored by Demeas' reaction, which Moschion was entirely unable to foresee. As Demeas quietly observes, Moschion is once again in the wrong. Whereas Demeas had sought to hide Moschion's error, Moschion's action will publicise his; whereas Demeas had sought to excuse Moschion on the basis of past conduct, Moschion apparently puts one day's wrong over a lifetime of kindness (706–10). Moschion has once again put himself in a position which threatens the play's happy resolution. Nikeratos' appearance releases this tension as once again Menander uses his presence to alter the tone of a scene. Nikeratos' ignorance of the true situation makes his abrupt questions comic, and his momentary loss of temper threatens a repetition of his earlier, overblown denunciations (715ff.). Similarly, his version of the

customary betrothal formula has an unexpected comic twist as
he promises a dowry only when he dies . . . which he hopes may
never happen (726–8). As in Act IV, Nikeratos' bluster saves
Moschion from making an embarrassing admission. All is at
last ready for the celebration, and Demeas again addresses the
audience directly, this time with the formal appeal for the
audience's favour that announces the play's close.

But what of Chrysis? Demeas' call to have her make the
necessary preparations draws attention to her silent presence in
this final tableau, and of course she gives the play its title. She
may have had a self-characterising monologue in the gap after
line 57, and the two scenes of expulsion so crucial to the action
derive power from the pathos of her bewilderment as she is
thrust from house to house clutching the baby.[12] In a larger
sense, the repeated nursing motif gives a certain prominence to
the otherwise invisible female influence on events. The chatter
of Moschion's old nurse first aroused Demeas' suspicions, and
the sight of the baby being suckled by Chrysis and Plangon
goaded the old men to action in turn. Similarly, isolated allusions to Nikeratos' household open a small window on domestic
arrangements and suggest a strong wife and an admirable
solidarity in the face of his impetuosity (421–6, 558–61). As in
the *Epitrepontes*, an infant is the catalyst that sets the action in
motion, and the woman's dilemma receives sensitive treatment. Yet these elements form only a background, and any
further questions suggested by them are strictly outside the
play: did Chrysis and Demeas resume their relationship as
before; what did Plangon think of Moschion; who raised the
baby? There is ample material here for a sub-plot, and Menander's refusal to develop one is a significant aspect of his technique.[13] It is not due to an inability or reluctance to create
strong female roles, for such women as Habrotonon of the
Epitrepontes and Glykera of the *Perikeiromene* certainly control
events. Rather, it is an indication of Menander's freedom in
using the situations from which he makes his play. Moschion
unwittingly becomes his own obstructor by concealing the
truth, and the resulting complications establish the obstructed
marriage situation as the play's primary source of action. The
disrupted union of Demeas and Chrysis is a momentary conse-

quence and is not expanded for its own sake. Woman and child are among the elements available for strengthening the development and impact of the main action, and Menander uses them freely without incurring any responsibility to grant them an independent, fully developed existence. We have seen how the lost water jar of the *Dyskolos* and Sikon's shortage of crockery become crucial to the action, while Knemon's daughter receives no name, Chaireas and Daos vanish from the scene, and Sostratos' sister is created out of thin air to provide a bride for Gorgias. Here in the *Samia*, though Chrysis' presence at the wedding celebration presumes a reconciliation with Demeas, its details are not the dramatist's concern, much as Nikeratos' scrawny sheep and leaky roof spice his characterization with comic hints of penury without developing a contrast of thematic significance with Demeas' wealth. Menander may be lavish in his use of situations to build or colour action, but he his highly selective in choosing which of them to develop.[14]

This freedom of choice raises a final question of dramatic priorities. The *Samia* combines subtle and broad humour, pathos and drama, comic convention and plausible motivation, but not in equal measure. Menander uses poignancy and characterisation as tools for making stock elements individual and memorable. The play may derive its greatest comic moments from a boy's conventional indiscretion and the familiar sight of raging old men, but by setting their actions against a background of poignancy and sympathy, he creates a unique effect. Moschion's foolishness stems from a heart-felt embarrassment. Demeas is moved to action by genuine anguish, while Chrysis' calm puts his anger in sharp relief. The pain of characters in the *Dyskolos* was largely external, caused by working in a field or falling down a well. Hints of mental turmoil are subordinate and, as we have seen, resolved mechanically. Unease in the *Samia* is internal. Moschion's reluctance to tell the truth and Demeas' misapprehension and fear for their relationship generate the action and control its direction from within. Menander dramatises their pain as comedy by juxtaposing against it the irony of their misunderstanding and the figure of Nikeratos as a consistently comic mirror of Demeas' anguish. This combination of serious motivation and comic action creates the inner tension that gives the play its interest and dramatic effect. It also suggests something further.

The play is a deliberate construction, and our investigation has led us to examine its material and the way Menander has chosen to arrange and join it. The obstructed marriage that provides a basic structure was furnished by the tradition; only the dramatist's ability to impart to it a diverse range of colorations makes the result truly original and intriguing. Yet the arrangement he chose is neither fixed nor inevitable. If the tradition is one of many elements, it is also one of many possibilities. Menander mixes the serious and the light, makes character a source of action, and subordinates one situation to another. Different priorities applied to the same set of elements may produce a play of quite different effect. But how do these plays actually work on an audience? How, to return to the terms of that famous and puzzling ancient epigram, do their rather formulaic actions convince us to see in them an imitation of life? Menander's legacy consists not simply of stockpiled materials for making plays, but of a dynamic model for their combination. The appeal of that model to later dramatists and audiences must be the focus of our conclusion.

VIII

Menander and Life

ὦ Μένανδρε καὶ βίε,
πότερος ἄρ' ὑμῶν πότερον ἀπεμιμήσατο;

Menander and life,
which of you imitated which?

Aristophanes of Byzantion (Test. 32 K–T)

Though the creative vigour and diversity of Aristophanes' art so often seize our attention, it was Menander, through the adaptations of Plautus and Terence, who exerted the greater influence on the shape of later western comedy. The components of his plays, with their wide appeal and flexibility, could nourish successors in a way that Aristophanic comedy could not do. A dramatist can make what he wishes of·them, while their association with the familiar ensures rapport between the audience and the action on the stage. The situations the tradition provides and the relationships they represent offer diverse possibilities for their dramatisation. Consider, for example, the motif of returning travellers. Young Sostratos returns from a journey in our fragment of the *Dis Exapaton* (*The Double Deception*), but Menander pays scant attention to the fact of his safe arrival. Emphasis is on his state of mind as he discovers the supposed unfaithfulness of his best friend and his mistress; the scene simply looks ahead to the confrontation with Moschos. At *Samia* 96ff. Menander lingers over the motif as he delineates the characters of Demeas and Nikeratos through dialogue concerning their return from Pontos. He highlights their situation by having baggage porters accompany them and by including an address to their homeland that was probably characteristic of returning travellers. The scene is brief but incorporates elements whose expansion John Wright has identified as typical of arrival scenes in Roman comedy. In turning the *Dis Exapaton* into his *Bacchis Girls*, for example, Plautus adds the baggage train Menander had withheld, and he has his young man greeted with an invitation to dinner (494ff.).[1] The traveller's address to his homeland, sometimes turned into explicit thanksgiving for a safe arrival, is frequently expanded in specifically Latin ways (e.g. *Stichus* 649–54, *Trinummus* 820–39). The bare necessity for an arrival has a potential for speech-making and spectacle that each dramatist can realize his own way.

A different kind of potential lies in the fixed backdrop, whose two or three doors make entrances and exits so easy to stage.[2] The doors are a convenient device, and the dramatist may well use them simply as a device. At *Dyskolos* 189ff. Knemon's daughter appears and vanishes into a house that is no more than a facade. Yet the dramatist may choose to give his setting depth and to indicate life going on beyond the door. There are several techniques. Characters direct speeches within, as Simiche and Getas do near the end of the *Dyskolos* (874–9). Simiche's speech recalls Knemon sulking in his house; Getas' remark to the sacrificers evokes the celebration going on in the shrine. The finale will involve Knemon's movement from one interior to the other, and the preparatory calls remind us of those off-stage events. Descriptive monologues such as Demeas' speech at *Samia* 219ff. bring alive the bustle of a household within. A third technique lies in a character's movement into his house and back. At *Samia* 516ff. the off-stage shouts and Nikeratos' feverish rushing to and fro bring to life the unseen figures of the nursing girl and strong-willed wife. When Nikeratos disappears inside, he is going to a real place. Plautus' *Miles Gloriosus* gives depth to the setting by having an interior action – a lovers' meeting made possible by a secret passage between adjoining houses – set the play's first intrigue in motion.[3] An off-stage cry of despair or perhaps of a woman in childbirth can also be used to make an unseen event more vivid, though of the ancient comic writers Terence is perhaps the least at ease with the device (cf. Simo's comments at *Andria* 474ff.).

The limited set of characters has its own potential, too, though we must distinguish between truly stock types and those more prone to individuality. Menander uses cooks, for example, as a comic pacing device in different plays by giving

them little more than the self-importance and verbosity characteristic of their type, but other figures have a more variable set
of traits. A Smikrines is generally a rather unpleasant old man
with an eye on money, but he need not be either a miser or a
villain. Smikrines of the *Aspis* is both, but Smikrines of the
Epitrepontes, though inclined toward financial pettiness, is not
an unsympathetic character. His concern for his daughter is
genuine, and the play's happy resolution depends upon his
ability to arbitrate a dispute justly. While Sikon of the *Dyskolos*
may be almost indistinguishable from the anonymous cooks of
the *Aspis* and *Samia*, these two Smikrines are distinct individuals. We might be tempted to include the military *alazon* in the
first category. Bias of Menander's *Fawner* (*Kolax*) was probably
a stock figure, and the *miles gloriosus* was always popular on the
Roman stage. The soldier, however, proved a more versatile
type than the cook. Menander gave his Polemon and
Thrasonides major, sympathetic roles that explore the soldier's
difficulty in adjusting to civilian life, and the Roman *miles*
showed great flexibility in his new surroundings. Terence got a
laugh by having his Thraso claim an old Roman stage joke as
an original witicism, and Plautus' Therapontigonus
Platagidorus and Pyrgopolynices, whose very names are a
Roman joke at the expense of Greek, model their lists of con-
quests on the form of Roman honorific inscriptions.[4] In the
Truculentus Plautus created still a different comic effect by having his Stratophanes, like Xanthias in *The Frogs*, criticize just
the type of joke the audience is expecting:

> Ne exspectetis, spectatores, meas pugnas dum praedicem:
> manibus duella praedicere soleo, haud in sermonibus.

> Spectators, don't expect me to proclaim my deeds of arms.
> I'm accustomed to proclaim my prowess with my hands, not with
>   words.   (482–3)

The themes of New Comedy are thus able to generate many
variations. This may partly explain the tradition's appeal to
dramatists, but what of its appeal to audiences? There is, of
course, considerable potential for humour. The concluding
fantasia of the *Dyskolos*, Sosias' militant rabble in the
Perikeiromene, and Chairestratos' feigned illness in the *Aspis* are

diverse sources of lively humour in Menander's comedy. At Rome the *comoedia palliata*, while rooted in the characters and plots of Greek New Comedy, developed its own style based upon special characteristics of the Latin language, independent traditions of mime and farce, and a deliberate mixing of Greek and Roman details. Eighteenth-century England turned similar romantic situations into witty, sometimes farcical plays of manners, and the humour of Wilde's *Earnest* depends in part upon the modern world's amused appreciation of an ancient mechanism. But the tradition can also turn a more serious side toward the audience. The suppressed recognition of *Lady Windermere's Fan* creates genuine poignancy, and Molière's Alceste is a far cry from his Scapin. Terence is often more austere than Plautus, and so is Menander, whose wry and sometimes broad humour is not the essence of his appeal. Tradition credits Aristophanes of Byzantion, a leading scholar in the century of Menander's death, with the famous epigram about Menander and Life imitating each other, and we must look to that imitative power for the source of New Comedy's more serious appeal.

How a writer sees and represents 'life' is shaped by the work of his predecessors and the conventions of his genre, but the writer's ability to refashion tradition reflects his own interests and talents. We expect a poet to show us something new, but his statement originates in the familiar. Thus Aristotle saw the tragic poet as a maker of plots, revealing character through the actions his tradition provides in outline. As Gerald Else comments, 'he is not invited to study his own soul and express things that never existed before, but to apprehend true types of human character and represent what they will do or say under given circumstances.'[5] In a well-known fragment from a play called *Poesis* (fr. 191 K) Antiphanes contrasts the tragedians' reliance on traditional material with the comic writers' supposed task. Put Oedipus on the stage, says Antiphanes, and the audience at once knows all about him, but the comic writer must 'invent everything: fresh names, situations past and present, the ending, the prologue.' Like all comic overstatement, Antiphanes' remark contains a grain of truth; a Chremes or Pheidon does not possess the crowd of associations that surround Oedipus or Adrastos. The knowledge and the attitude towards myth and legend that shaped the audience's response to tragedy do find an equivalent, however, in the recurrent names, situations, and devices of New Comedy. Though this material is not grand, it is familiar, and like the tragic poets, Menander reworks it to reveal something new. Moschion and Demeas begin the *Samia* in familiar roles, but as the play progresses they become distinct individuals who learn specific lessons. So do Charisios of the *Epitrepontes*, Polemon and Thrasonides of the *Perikeiromene* and *Misoumenos*, and to some extent even Knemon of the *Dyskolos*. We respond to them as individuals, and through our response Menander is able to touch us.

His ability to generate this response may seem to be in spite of limitations inherent in his chosen medium. Some such limitations are imposed by the nature of play-making itself. The dramatist, for example, unlike the novelist, cannot take us inside a character's mind except through what the character himself says or what others say about him.[6] Opportunities for omniscient portrayal are severely restricted and even soliloquy – so potent a tool for Shakespeare and Racine – is limited to the character's conscious knowledge of his mental state and his powers of self-expression. Menander sometimes surmounts this difficulty by turning ostensible narrative monologues, such as Moschion's prologue to the *Samia*, into self-portraits by the character's unconscious ordering of his thoughts and the language in which he expresses them. A play, though, can support only a limited number of such speeches, and the dramatist's main recourse must be dialogue. Thus Smikrines' greed in the *Aspis*, which Tyche makes explicit, is revealed first by his questioning of Daos and later confirmed by his insistence on a formal inventory of Kleostratos' estate. Dialogue with Pataikos reveals Polemon's innocent simplicity in the third act of the *Perikeiromene*. Knemon's long speech at *Dyskolos* 713ff. is perhaps as close as Menander comes to making a character's mental state explicit, and the desire to work it into a dramatic context limits both its length and complexity. The acting conventions of Menander's time imposed a different kind of limitation. The naturalistic style of acting introduced by David

Garrick in the eighteenth century could enliven many plays
whose formulaic scripts tended toward flatness. Audiences
thrilled to what a contemporary account called 'th' expressive
features, and the speaking eye' with which his vibrant personality convinced them to see in such plays a mirror of life.[7]
Menander could not rely on his actors' personal mannerisms or
on the plasticity of their features. His theatre was too large and
ancient acting put vocal resonance and diction first. With
features hidden by the masks and single roles divided among
members of the company, there was little opportunity for an
actor to project his personality into a role. A plausible scheme
for the distribution of parts in the *Dyskolos*, for example,
requires two actors to divide the part of Sostratos, including his
major monologues, between them.[8] Gestures were broad, and
the desire to project the voice no doubt encouraged actors to
speak dialogue 'out front' rather than to each other. The
Mytilene mosaics, which date from the third century of our own
era, represent scenes of lively action with the broad gestures
and uniform staging we perceive as highly conventionalised
performance.

But the conventions of New Comedy are also a source of
power. They limit the dramatist to an established set of techniques, but the audience's knowledge of them is an important
tool for the dramatist's creativity. We have seen, for example,
how Menander can build upon expectations by reworking
conventions and mixing modes. The resulting effects depend on
both the text he writes and on how he knows his audience will
perceive that text when performed. The audience brings something to the play. Domestic drama evokes not only their memory of theatrical tradition, but their own experience of family
life. That scene in Terence with which this study began was
based upon a Menandrean original and provides a convenient
example of the resulting interplay.

The action of *The Andrian Girl* turns upon a favourite situation of Roman comedy. Young Pamphilus loves the Andrian
girl Glycerium, who has borne his child in the course of the
play, but Pamphilus' father Simo insists he marry their neighbour's daughter. Only the unexpected discovery that
Glycerium is an Attic citizen, a lost daughter of the neighbour

Chremes, resolves the impasse. In the last act, as the recognition mechanism begins to move, Simo at first refuses to believe the story, and his suspicion and irritation lead to an explosive confrontation with his son.

> ain tandem, civi' Glyceriumst? :: ita praedicant.
> :: 'ita praedicant'? o ingentem confidentiam!
> num cogitat quid dicat? num facti piget?

> You also claim Glycerium is a citizen, do you? :: So they say.
> :: 'So they say'? What immense cheek!
> Does he think what he's saying? Does the deed shame him?
>
> (875–7)

When confronted with Simo's bald statement of the alleged fact, Pamphilus tries to hedge, and that hedging is too much for Simo. In agony over the apparent realization of his worst fears, Simo then tries to dismiss Pamphilus entirely from his mind.

> quor meam senectutem huius sollicito amentia?
> an ut pro huius peccatis ego supplicium sufferam?
> immo habeat, valeat, vivat cum illa. :: mi pater!
> :: quid 'mi pater'? quasi tu huius indigeas patris.

> Why harras my old age with his foolishness?
> Should I suffer torment for his faults?
> Let him keep her, go off with her, live with her. :: Father!
> :: What 'father'? As if you needed this father.   (887–90)

Pamphilus responds with a confession that is a masterful combination of filial piety and loyalty to Glycerium.

> tibi, pater, me dedo; quidvis oneris inpone, impera.
> vis me uxorem ducere? hanc vis mittere? ut potero feram.

> I put myself in your hands, father. Impose what burden you
>   choose. Order me.
> You want me to marry? You want me to send this girl away? I'll
>   bear it as best I can.   (897–8)

His surrender is nearly total; only the 'ut potero' reminds us of his still divided loyalties.

This scene, built from a stereotyped situation and the stock figures of angry father and young lover, nevertheless generates considerable power. A sensitivity to human emotion lifts it above stereotype. Simo's lapses into the third person are deliberate efforts to divorce Pamphilus from his thoughts and his responsibility. He is attempting to put distance between himself and his son, and the words convey a bitterness and resignation which Pamphilus' honesty tries to soften. The humility and respect of his reply prevent the fuming father from being absurd. Pamphilus takes him seriously, and Simo's willingness to hear this confession suggests a genuine hesitation on his part to make the breach complete. The emergence of the truth will eventually bring father and son back together, but not before they have reached the brink of an emotional abyss. The signs of this tension are deft and subtle; the sudden change of person, the earnestness, the anguished exclamations. These are genuine outbursts of feeling rather than unbridled raving, and both characters are totally caught up in the emotion of the confrontation. Even Chremes, a largely silent witness to their exchange, is moved by it. Yet Terence's language plays down the drama, and he can afford to let it do so because he has a silent ally in his audience's perceptions. In presenting a father and son at loggerheads Terence is creating a scene as familiar in everyday life as in drama. He is alluding to emotions and responses we have experienced ourselves. The tragic poet cannot depend upon his audience to know how it feels to be Oedipus or Orestes. That is one reason why tragedy draws upon the language and imagery of high poetry for some of its impact, but Terence can rely on the plain-spoken confrontation of Simo and Pamphilus to create sympathetic vibrations in an audience composed of parents and children. Simo's anger and Pamphilus' anguish strike us as 'real' not simply because of what Terence has them say, but because of what we bring to the scene as witnesses.

Drama's power to imitate life – or to make life seem to imitate drama – has a double source: what the dramatist presents and what the audience perceives. It is in the very nature of imitation (*mimesis*) to be a process of perception as well as a process of creation. A short discussion in the second book of Philostratos' *Life of Apollonios of Tyana*, written early in the third century AD, emphasizes this duality. The sage Apollonios and his follower Damis discuss painting and soon turn their attention to the images we sometimes see in the clouds. Are these also products of imitation? Surely not, for 'these figures flit through the heaven . . . by mere chance; while we who by nature are prone to imitation rearrange and create them in these regular figures.' Even if we drew an Indian in white chalk, says Apollonios, his flat nose, stiff curling hair, and prominent jaw would cause us to perceive him as black. 'Those who look at works of painting and drawing', he concludes, 'require a mimetic faculty; for no one could appreciate or admire a picture of a horse or a bull, unless he had formed an idea of the creature represented.'[9]

When Aristophanes of Byzantion asked of Menander and Life which had imitated the other, he was playing upon the widely held belief that it was indeed the function of art to imitate life. Aristotle assumes at the outset of *The Poetics* that all art is mimetic, and so did Plato in *Republic* 10. What ancient writers actually meant by *mimesis*, however, remains something of a problem. The value of this passage in Philostratos, which has been largely ignored in the scholarly discussion, is that it directs our attention to the underlying question: what actual phenomenon were ancient literary theorists seeking to describe by the terms *mimesis* and *mimeisthai*? The primary sense of the verb *mimeisthai* in the fifth century BC was to mime or to mimic and had the specific connotation of *mimos*, the actual art form of the mime. From this developed the meaning 'to imitate' in a general sense, and the slightly later nouns *mimema* and *mimesis* transferred the concept from actions to images.[10] Mimicry, of course, does not require fully detailed imitation. An adept mimic can choose a few salient features and by reproducing these suggest the entirety to his audience. This is how a modern political cartoonist makes a ski-jump nose represent an American president regardless of the face he puts behind it and how Apollonios' hypothetical artist could draw a black Indian in white chalk. Truly representational art, if so we may distinguish 'serious' art from caricature, may depict a man in profile with only one shoulder and a foreshortened arm, but if done correctly we will perceive the resulting figure as more 'realistic' than, say, an ancient Egyptian figure drawn with the two shoulders and two arms of equal length that we know it actually must possess. Such examples are fairly straightforward, and it is not hard to see why both Plato and Aristotle often resorted to the example of painting to explain their meaning by analogy (e.g. *Rep.* 596e, *Soph.* 234b; *Poet.* 1448a5–6, 54b8–14). The dramatist's task, however, is to imitate not simply figures but figures in action. How does he do so? The painter's limitation may suggest the dramatist's strength.

When Socrates asked the painter Parrhasios if he could imitate the disposition of the soul, Parrhasios immediately replied that he could not imitate that which had neither shape nor colour and was invisible. The artist may suggest more than he shows, but his craft limits his representation to line and tone. 'Nature', observes E. H. Gombrich, 'cannot be imitated or "transcribed" without first being taken apart and put together again,' and the painter's ability to do so is limited by his medium and by the beholder's power to read his message.[11] Dramatic art is also a process of analysis and the translation of nature into the terms of its medium. The dramatist, however, has a larger set of tools for suggesting what he cannot represent directly. The visual aspect of stage performance is, as Aristotle perceived, only a small part of what the audience experiences. Ancient drama in particular, whose pivotal actions generally took place off the stage, depended upon character, thought, and language to make their significance manifest to its audience. Remember the confrontation scene of *The Andrian Girl*. A conflict between father and son is an established part of the comic tradition, as are both Pamphilus' rather mindless love for Glycerium and Simo's weakness for outbursts of temper. The situation could hardly be more artificial. This particular scene strikes us as true, as a genuine representation of what a father and son feel and say, because of the way Terence has translated the phenomenon from life to the stage. The thoughts that underlie their statements, what Aristotle called *dianoia*, make the scene and are of Terence's own creation.[12] Simo's effort to dismiss Pamphilus from his mind and Pamphilus' sudden fear of antagonizing his father beyond redress are the salient features of actual father–son conflicts that Terence has chosen to suggest 'real life', and by capturing these he gives the entire scene the ring of truth.

We saw something similar in the last act of Menander's

Samia. The final confrontation between Moschion and Demeas begins as stock comedy. The slapstick scene with Parmenon established the essentially comic nature of Moschion's scheme to punish his father, and the younger man's anxious pacing before the door is more absurd than tense. Demeas' short, indignant questions as he leaves the house looking for Moschion seem to promise just the loud confrontation Moschion hopes to provoke. All expectations are confounded, however, by Demeas' sudden change of tone as he takes in the situation. His speech becomes soft-spoken, without signs either of impatience or circumlocution. He is serious and honest, and the result is a sudden surge of real sympathy, perhaps the first in the play, for Moschion. By treating his father with less consideration than he has received, he earns the reproach he has feared since the beginning, but it comes in the form of a plea. Of all the possible responses Demeas could make, Menander has chosen just the one to cast Moschion's error in sharpest relief and turn his comic bravado into a discomfort worthy of our sympathy. Demeas' simply expressed confession reveals the events of the play to be no mechanical chain of comic misunderstandings, but a series of very human errors that has not left him unscathed. His speech implies more than it says, and this sudden glimpse of true feeling colours our understanding of the entire scene.

Our perception of a scene as 'lifelike' is thus actually a response to specific features chosen for their ability to evoke the whole. This brings us back to Socrates and Parrhasios and ultimately to Aristophanes of Byzantion. Both touch upon the same phenomenon and apply to it the same verb, *apomimeisthai*. Socrates' further discussion with Parrhasios showed that since facial expressions suggest mental states, Parrhasios could indeed paint a portrait that revealed its subject as happy or sad, generous or mean, and so good or bad. By painting eyes, mouth, or forehead in a certain way he can make these specific details suggest the idea of character to the beholder. The painter translates the abstract into the concrete, and we, as we view the work, read the abstract concept in the visual signs. Though Socrates does not make it explicit, this is the process he has in mind. The compound verb *apomimeisthai* itself hints at the idea of transferral.[13] Aristophanes of Byzantion was a scholar, and he read Menander with a scholar's keen eye for language.[14] His sensitivity to linguistic subtlety enabled him to perceive Menander's skill in transferring human emotion to the dramatic medium, and he also denoted the process of successful transferral by the verb *apomimeisthai*. But what did he mean by life (*bios*)?

Aristotle's statement that tragedy is an imitation of life came as an expansion of his basic tenet that tragedy represents men in action: 'for tragedy is the imitation not of men but of actions and of life . . .' (*Poet.* 1450a16–17). As Gerald Else remarks, '"Life" tends to connote to us the vastness, complexity, unpredictability, inexhaustible variety, etc. of the human scene,' but Aristotle's sense is more restricted. Drama is action of a comparatively spare kind and depicts not the diversity of the human scene but the way of life or perhaps, as Else suggests, the careers of a set of characters.[15] Though in later antiquity *bios* did expand its connotations, there was still nothing grandiose about it. Aristotle's student and intellectual heir Theophrastos apparently characterized tragedy as heroic (ἡρωϊκῶς) and comedy as ordinary (βιωτικῶς). The grammarian Dionysios Thrax, a pupil of Aristarchos and thus direct heir to the tradition of Aristophanes of Byzantion, makes the distinction explicit, and it is expanded by a commentator on Dionysios who suggests he used βιωτικῶς κατὰ μίμησις βίου, 'because tragedy is an account and recital of events that happened, but comedy embraces images of everyday affairs'. The same tradition is reflected in Donatus' report that Cicero called comedy 'an imitation of life, a mirror of manners, an image of truth' ('imitationem vitae, speculum consuetudinis, imaginem veritatis').[16] This connotation of everyday life singles comedy out as the particular *mimesis biou* and helps explain, for example, why Mercury takes such pains to excuse the presence of gods and heroes in Plautus' *Amphitruo* (50–96). As the grammarian Diomedes put it, 'comedy differs from tragedy in that tragedy introduces heroes, leaders and kings, while comedy [represents] humble and private individuals' (XXIV.2 Koster).

But the rapes, recognitions and rages that generate so much of the action in Menander's comedies are no everyday occurrences. The plays may represent the hopes and fears of Athenians in the politically unstable fourth century, but surely not the events of their actual lives.[17] Yet, as we have seen, the response of his characters to those sometimes extraordinary situations is consistently keyed to the familiar responses of ordinary people. The atypical situations excite interest and make possible the self-contained plots, but their oddity is ultimately less significant than their familiarity. The circumstances of Charisios' separation from his wife in the *Epitrepontes* are highly unusual, not to say improbable, and incorporate the seeds of a happy resolution with a fortuitous economy real life seldom duplicates. Charisios' *response* is what we recognize as being really true to life. His anguish, his shifting of blame to his wife, and his eventual shame mirror the responses of actual people to their own more ordinary, though analogous crises. This similarity of response is the aspect of 'true' life that Menander captures in his plays, and our recognition of that truth makes the difficulties of Charisios, of Polemon, of Moschion and Demeas so engrossing. Only a small piece of Life is imitated on Menander's stage, and only a small piece is necessary. Our own response does the rest.

The set of conventions that was Greek New Comedy has enjoyed its long and varied history because of the opportunities it offers dramatists and the diverse responses it elicits from audiences. 'Man spricht immer von Originalität,' Goethe once complained to Eckermann, 'allein was will das sagen! . . . was können wir denn unser Eigenes nennen, als die Energie, die Kraft, das Wollen!'[18] Menander's originality lies not primarily in the building blocks of his comedy, for these lay at hand in the tradition, but in his use of them. The making of comedy is a dynamic process, and Menander's powers of combination demonstrated the versatility of his components to generations of successors. Energy, power, and a clearly perceived intention are indeed the tools with which he worked his material, and the success of his effort can be read on nearly every page, however fragmentary, of the comedies he made.

Bibliography

An extensive critical bibliography covering work on Menander from 1955 to 1973 has been compiled by H. J. Mette, *Lustrum* 10 (1965) 5–211, 11 (1966) 139–43, 13 (1968) 535–68, and 16 (1971/72) 5–80. Also of value are the review essays by A. Dain, *Maia* 15 (1963) 278–309 and W. G. Arnott, *Menander, Plautus, Terence* [Greece and Rome New Surveys in the Classics No. 9 (Oxford 1975)]. Translations include L. Casson, *The Plays of Menander* (New York 1971) and a Penguin edition, now somewhat out of date, by P. Vellacott, *Menander, Plays and Fragments* (London 1973). The first volume of a new edition by W. G. Arnott in the Loeb Classical Library series will appear in 1979. The essays in the *Fondation Hardt Entretiens XVI* (Geneva 1970) are indispensable for the student of Menander, as is A. W. Gomme and F. H. Sandbach, *Menander, A Commentary* (Oxford 1973). E. W. Handley, *The Dyskolos of Menander* (London 1965) contains much information of general interest, especially on metre and theatrical conventions. For monographs and papers on individual plays, consult the notes to the preceding chapters. The following works are also helpful:

Literary History

Arnim, H. von, 'Kunst und Weisheit in den Komödien Menanders', *Neue Jahrbücher fur das klassische Altertum* 25 (1910) 241–53.

Arnott, W. G., 'From Aristophanes to Menander', *G&R* 19 (1972) 65–80.

—, 'Menander, qui vitae ostendit vitam', *G&R* 15 (1968) 1–17.

Burck, E., 'Die Kunst Menanders und ihre Bedeutung für die Entwicklung der Komödie', *Neue Jahrbücher* NF 9 (1933) 417–31.

Dover, K. J., 'Greek Comedy' in *Fifty Years (and Twelve) of Classical Scholarship* (Oxford 1968) 123–58.

Fantham, E., 'Sex, Status and Survival in Hellenistic Athens: A Study of Women in New Comedy', *Phoenix* 29 (1975) 44–74.

Fauth, W., 'Kulinarisches und Utopisches in der griechischen Komödie', *WS* 7 (1973) 39–62.

Flashar, H., 'Zur Eigenart des aristophanischen Spätwerks', *Poetica* 1

(1967) 154–75 = H. -J. Newiger, ed. *Aristophanes und die Alte Komödie* (Darmstadt 1975) 405–34.
Gaiser, K., 'Menander und der Peripatos', *A&A* 13 (1967) 8–40.
Gomme, A. W., 'Menander' in *Essays in Greek History and Literature* (Oxford 1937) 249–95.
Legrand, P. E., *The New Greek Comedy*, tr. J. Loeb (London 1917).
Lever, K., *The Art of Greek Comedy* (London 1956).
Maurach, G., 'Interpretationen zur attischen Komödie', *AClass* 11 (1968) 1–24.
Ricciardelli Apicella, G., 'Epicuro e Menandro', *RCCM* 10 (1968) 3–26.
Sandbach, F. H., *The Comic Theatre of Greece and Rome* (London 1977).
Webster, T. B. L., *An Introduction to Menander* (Manchester 1974).
Wehrli, F., *Motivstudien zur griechischen Komödie* (Zurich 1936).

Dramatic Technique

Arnott, W. G., 'A Note on the Motif of Eavesdropping Behind the Door in Comedy', *RhM* 108 (1965) 371–6.
—, 'Time, Plot and Character in Menander', *Papers of the Liverpool Latin Seminar*, vol. 2 (Liverpool 1979).
Bader, E., 'The Ψόφος of the House Door in Greek New Comedy', *Antichthon* 5 (1971) 35–48.
Bain, D., *Actors and Audience* (Oxford 1977).
Görler, W., Über die Illusion in der antiken Komödie', *A&A* 18 (1973) 41–57.
Oliva, C., 'La parodia e la critica letteraria nella commedia post-aristofanea', *Dioniso* 42 (1968) 25–92.
Sandbach, F. H., 'Menander and the Three-Actor Rule', *Le monde Grec . . . Hommages à Claire Préaux* (Brussels 1975) 197–204.
Webster, T. B. L., 'Menander: Production and Imagination', *Bull. John Rylands Lib.* 45 (1962/63) 235–72.

Language and Metre

Del Corno, D., 'Alcuni aspetti del linguaggio di Menandro', *SCO* 24 (1975) 13–48.
Descroix, J., *Le trimètre iambique* (Paris 1931).
Feneron, J., 'Some Elements of Menander's Style', *BICS* 21 (1974) 81–95.
Flury, P., *Liebe und Liebessprache bei Menander, Plautus und Terenz* (Heidelberg 1968).

Perusino, F., 'Tecnica e stile nel tetrametro trocaico di Menandro', *RCCM* 4 (1962) 45–64.
—, Il tetrametro giambico catalettico (Rome 1968).
Zini, S., *Il linguaggio dei personaggi nelle commedie di Menandro* (Florence 1938).

Stock Characters

Arnott, W. G., 'Alexis and the Parasite's Name', *GRBS* 9 (1968) 161–8.
Dohm, H., *Mageiros* (Munich 1964).
Giannini, A., 'La figura del cuoco nella commedia greca', *Acme* 13 (1961) 135–217.
Gigante, M., 'Il ritorno del medico straniero', *PP* 24 (1969) 302–7.
Gil, L. and Alfageme, I. R., 'La figura del médico en la comedia ática', *CFC* 3 (1972) 35–91.
Guardì, T., 'I precendenti greci della figura del *servus currens* della commedia romana', *Pan* 2 (1974) 5–15.
Harsh, P. W., 'The Intriguing Slave in Greek Comedy', *TAPA* 86 (1955) 135–42.
Hauschild, C. H., *Die Gestalt der Hetäre in der griechischen Komödie* (Leipzig 1933).
MacCary, W. T., 'Menander's Characters: Their Names, Roles and Masks', *TAPA* 101 (1970) 277–90.
Oeri, H. G., *Der Typ der komischen Alten in der griechischen Komödie* (Basel 1948).

Notes

CHAPTER I

1 For the distinct structure of Old Comedy see F. H. Sandbach, *The Comic Theatre of Greece and Rome* (London 1977) 42–5 and the introduction to W. B. Stanford's edition of *The Frogs* (London 1971) xlv–xlix.

2 The development of post-Aristophanic comedy is surveyed by Sandbach (above, note 1) 55–75. K. Lever, *The Art of Greek Comedy* (London 1956) 160–85 lets the plays speak for themselves through liberal quotation. There is unfortunately no translation of the Greek comic fragments available in English except J. M. Edmonds, *The Fragments of Attic Comedy*, 3 vols. in 4 (Leiden 1957–61), which is unreliable in both Greek text and translation. The best technical discussion remains that of A. Körte, *RE* 11.1 (1921) 1256–66, s.v. Komödie (Mittlere).

3 The authoritative accounts of these developments and of the character of Athenian theatrical performances are two volumes by A. W. Pickard-Cambridge, *The Theatre of Dionysus at Athens* (Oxford 1946) and *The Dramatic Festivals of Athens*, 2 ed. (Oxford 1968). Less technical are P. A. Arnott, *Greek Scenic Conventions in the Fifth Century B.C.* (Oxford 1962) and C. W. Dearden, *The Stage of Aristophanes* (London 1976).

4 Theophrastos, *Characters* 11.3; Plutarch, *Moralia* 674b–c. Xenophon speaks of Kallipides in his *Symposion* 3.11, and the remark about the *Kresphontes* is at *Moralia* 998e.

5 I quote the version of Dudley Fitts in his translation of *Frogs* 304. The error in Greek, at *Orestes* 279, was to mispronounce an acute accent as a circumflex, so that the audience heard 'ferret', the common Athenian housepet, instead of 'calm'. The slip was also ridiculed by Strattis, frs. 1 and 60K, by Sannyrion, fr. 8K, and in a lost play by the writer known to us as Plato Comicus.

6 Discussions of Greek metrics become technical with alarming speed, but see T. Rosenmeyer *et al.*, *The Metres of Greek and Latin Poetry* (London 1963), which includes a helpful glossary of technical terms. The extant plays of Menander contain iambic and trochaic tetrameters in addition to the predominant trimeter. See E. W. Handley, ed., *The Dyskolos of Menander* (London 1965) 56–73. Of great value for understanding the listener's perception of metre is the linguistic orientation of W. S. Allen, *Accent and Rhythm* (Cambridge 1973), e.g. 304–14 on the iambic trimeter.

7 The most comprehensive and lucid discussion of papyrus and its study is E. G. Turner, *Greek Papyri, An Introduction* (Oxford 1968).

8 E. G. Turner, *Greek Manuscripts of the Ancient World* (Oxford/Princeton 1971) 8–16 offers a succinct discussion of layout and punctuation keyed to the excellent plates of ancient books that follow.

CHAPTER II

1 In the second century AD the grammarian Julius Pollux described forty-four masks he claimed represented all the roles of New Comedy. Though we cannot verify the accuracy of his list for productions in Menander's own time, it has certainly proven valuable for identifying the many masks depicted on ancient vases and terracottas. See A. W. Pickard-Cambridge, *The Dramatic Festivals of Athens*, 2 ed. (Oxford 1968) 223–31, which includes excellent illustrations. W. T. MacCary 'Menander's Characters: Their Names, Roles and Masks', *TAPA* 101 (1970) 277–90 argues for the identification of names and character types in Menander with specific masks on Pollux' list.

2 G. F. Else, *Aristotle's Poetics: The Argument* (Cambridge, Mass. 1957) 8–9 emphasizes Aristotle's interest in craft and offers 'poetic process' as a translation of *poiesis* in the first sentence of *The Poetics*: 'how the plots should be constructed if the poetic process is to be artistically satisfactory . . .' The Greek word *poiētēs* itself means 'maker'.

3 W. N. Bates, *Euripides* (Philadelphia 1930) 17–21 gathers the evidence for Euripides' popularity in the fourth century; for his standing in his own time see P. T. Stevens, 'Euripides and the Athenians', *JHS* 76 (1956) 87–94.

4 A. P. Burnett, *Catastrophe Survived* (Oxford 1971) 16. Cf. L. Salingar, *Shakespeare and the Traditions of Comedy* (Cambridge 1974) 5: 'a stage convention, such as a familiar twist in a plot, is an expressive sign, a means of communication, between playwrights who use it and the audiences who enjoy or at least accept it.' For more on Euripides' daring see W. G. Arnott, 'Euripides and the Unexpected', *G&R* 20 (1973) 49–64 and B. M. W. Knox, 'Euripidean Comedy', in *The Rarer Action*, ed. A. Cheuse & R. Koffler (New Brunswick, N. J. 1970) 68–96.

5 The example is taken with slight modification from E. Fraenkel, *De media et nova comoedia quaestiones selectae* (Göttingen 1912) 59–63. Other adaptations discussed by Fraenkel include various forms of narrative soliloquy (32–53) and the end pattern of dramatic impasse and resolution (63–70). The use of sound to announce an entrance has been re-examined by B. Bader, 'The Ψόφος of the House-Door in Greek New Comedy', *Antichthon* 5 (1971) 35–48.

6 The Oxford edition of Menander puts Daos' words in quotation marks; G–S 742 expresses cogent doubts. For the audience's ability to recognize the tragic echoes and quotations in Aristophanes see R. M. Harriott,

'Aristophanes' Audience and the Plays of Euripides', *BICS* 9 (1962) 1–8 and P. Walcot, 'Aristophanic and Other Audiences', *G&R* 18 (1971) 35–50.

7 The structuralist É. Souriau, *Les deux cent mille situations dramatiques* (Paris 1950) 38, therefore defines a dramatic situation as 'la forme intrinsèque du système de forces qu'incarnent les personnages, à un moment donné étant bien entendu que ces forces résident dans les personnages et sont en eux; mais que d'autre part elles les transcendent, les dépassent, les surmontent ou les surplombent . . .'

8 This operational definition is distinct from the more philosophical 'theory of modes' developed by N. Frye, *Anatomy of Criticism* (Princeton 1957) 33–67. His modes centre on the external relationship between author and audience and are thus blueprints of meaning. Mine describe the relationship between the author and his material and as such are blueprints of mechanics.

9 This lack of affectation perhaps tells against R. Merkelbach's clever conjecture οὐκ ἀγρόθεν πυλῶν ἔσω (not from the country to the city gates) at 176. Contrast a fragment of Alkaios' *Komoidotragoidia* (fr. 19K):

ἐτύγχανον μὲν ἀγρόθεν πλείστους φέρων
εἰς τὴν ἑορτὴν ὅσον οἷον εἴκοσι,
ὁρῶ δ' ἄνωθεν γάργαρ' ἀνθρώπων κύκλῳ.

cf. *Or* 871: ὁρῶ δ' ὄχλον στείχοντα καὶ θάσσοντ' ἄκραν.

I happened to be bringing lots for a feast
up from the country – a good twenty or so —
and I see below a pile of people in a crowd.

cf. *Or* 871: I see a crowd approaching and someone sitting on a rise.

Here the interjected preparations for a feast, a common motif in comedy of the early fourth century, and substitution of the colloquial 'pile of people' for Euripides' 'crowd' are deliberately comic and, especially in a play of this title, suggest parody. The use of *kyklos*, commonly used by tragedians for an assembly or crowd, may be intended to make the entire phrase absurd. For the parallels between *Sikyonios* and *Orestes* see A. Katsouris, *Tragic Patterns in Menander* (Athens 1975) 29–54.

10 C. Whitman, *Aristophanes and the Comic Hero* (Cambridge, Mass. 1964) 261–2. A. W. Gomme, 'Menander' in *Essays in Greek History and Literature* Oxford 1937) 265–8 discusses Menander's tendency to restrict improbabilities of plot to the narration of preliminaries.

11 In introducing this scene, G–S 63 reads: 'Daos enters, followed by a crowd of captives, men and girls, and baggage animals . . .' Professor Sandbach has since pointed out to me how much more effective the scene would be if the baggage train entered first and the procession culminated with Daos' appearance. I follow his revised interpretation here.

12 K. J. Dover, *Aristophanic Comedy* (London 1972) 56. The most provocative discussion of the problem is W. Görler, 'Über die Illusion in der antiken Komödie', *A&A* 18 (1973) 41–57, which begins with the observation that

the Greeks had no word for 'dramatic illusion' and proceeds to show the varying relationships a play can create with its audience.

CHAPTER III

1 C. Goldoni, *Memoirs*, trans. J. Black (New York 1926) 222. N. Frye, *Anatomy of Criticism* (Princeton 1957) 178–9 observes that in ironic comedy such as this 'the demonic world is never far away.'

2 Examples are legion. See C. Oliva 'La parodia e la critica litteraria nella commedia post-aristofanea', *Dioniso* 42 (1968) 25–92.

3 The purpose of this law, the simple statement of which is probably more cruel than its actual practice, was to keep property in the family. For the procedure and its rationale see W. K. Lacey, *The Family in Classical Greece* (London 1968) 139–45 and A. R. W. Harrison, *The Laws of Athens*, vol. 1 (Oxford 1968) 132–8. The specific legal questions raised by the *Aspis* are discussed by E. Karabelias, 'Une nouvelle source pour l'étude du droit attique: Le 'Bouclier' de Ménandre', *Rev. hist. de droit fran. et étranger* 48 (1970) 357–89.

4 C. Whitman, *Aristophanes and the Comic Hero* (Cambridge, Mass. 1964) 25.

5 See the evidence gathered by L. Gil and I. R. Alfageme, 'La figura del médico en la comedia ática', *CFC* 3 (1972) 35–91. Doric roots are suggested by a papyrus from Oxyrhynchus (P. Oxy. 2659), a list of comic poets and their plays which credits a certain Dinolochos, a disciple or rival of the fifth-century Sicilian master Epicharmos, with a play called *Iatros*. E. G. Turner, 'A Fragment of Epicharmos?' *WS* 10 (1976) 45–57 offers a metrical text in the style of Epicharmos in which a doctor appears to be expounding, but whether it is a fragment of comedy remains uncertain. See the additional comments of E. W. Handley, 57–60.

6 For full discussion of the tragic echoes in this scene see D. B. Lombard, 'New Values in Traditional Form. A Study in Menander's *Aspis*', *A Class* 14 (1971) 123–45.

7 For standard jokes on cooks' propensity for theft, see H. Dohm, *Mageiros* (Munich 1964) 129–34. It should perhaps be noted that the cook's parody of tragic messengers here is more lexical than metrical. The scansion of his lines is permissible but not common in tragedy and thus not immediately tragic sounding. The parody depends upon the vocabulary and his own pompous manner.

8 Tertullian, *De anima* 20.3, discussing national characteristics, remarked 'comici Phrygas timidos illudunt'. Cf. Apollodoros, fr. 6K:

I am not entirely a Phrygian. If I saw that to die
was better than to live, I would endure the better.

R. K. Sherk, 'Daos and Spinther in Menander's *Aspis*', *AJP* 91 (1970) 341–3 cites the proverbs Φρὺξ ἀνὴρ πληγεὶς ἀμείνων καὶ διακονέστερος ('A beaten Phrygian is a better man and more compliant.') and Φρὺξ μηδὲν ἥττων Σπινθάρου ('A Phrygian is no worse than a Spinther = Spark.'), particulary appropriate in view of Menander's gratuitous name for the cook's assistant. On the virility and bravado of Thracians cf. Menander, fr. 794–5 and 805K–T. I am grateful to Professor Timothy Long, who is currently investigating the role of barbarians in Greek comedy, for his help in identifying these *topoi*. Such characterizations are not inconsistent with the representation of barbarians in Euripidean tragedy, e.g. *Andr.* 215ff. (the marriage customs of Thrace) and *Or.* 1110–14, 1507ff. (the decadance of Phrygians). See the discussion of these passages by H. Bacon, *Barbarians in Greek Tragedy* (New Haven Conn. 1961) 145–8, and now T. Long, 'Menander's *Aspis* 206–8,' *Hermes* 107 (1979) 117–18.

9 For the hearing, called an *epidikasia*, see Harrison (above, n. 3) 9–12; Karabelias (above, n. 3) 364–8 discusses the concept of *kyrieia* in the *Aspis*. The family relationships of the play must be inferred from the text, e.g. G–S 76–7. They are not made explicit.

10 D. Del Corno, 'Ancora sull' *Aspis* di Menandro', *ZPE* 8 (1971) 29–32 argues that Chairestratos collapses *outside* the house in view of the audience and cites as a parallel Euripides' *Hecuba* 438ff. (Hecuba loses Polyxena and collapses). A. G. Katsouris, *Tragic Patterns in Menander* (Athens 1975) 108 n. 2 concurs, but G–S *ad loc.* argues instead that Daos' voice is heard from behind the *skene* at 299, first addressing Chairestratos and then calling out to Chaireas. This is probably the correct interpretation. Two arguments can be made against Del Corno and Katsouris: (1) sight of Chairestratos' collapse would distract attention from Chaireas' monologue, and (2) it would make Daos' lines 299–300 largely superfluous. Daos is in effect describing what has happened to Chairestratos, a standard technique for representing *unseen* action. See A. M. Dale, 'Seen and Unseen on the Greek Stage', *WS* 69 (1956) 96–106 = *Collected Papers* (Cambridge 1969) 119–29.

11 Plautine expansion of the slave's role was appreciated by F. Leo, *Geschichte der römischen Literatur*, vol. 1 (Berlin 1913) 144–5 and merits a chapter in E. Fraenkel, *Elementi plautini in Plauto*, tr. F. Munari (Florence 1960) 223–41. Military imagery appears at the beginning of Menander's *Perikeiromene* and in the Act II dialogue between Moschion and Daos, but there it is shared between them and the figure of the soldier Polemon, central to the action makes it anything but gratuitous.

12 P. Oxy. 11, lines 30–1 (Austin no. 254), cf. Terence *Andr.* 206: 'Enimvero, Dave, nil locist segnitiae neque secordiae.' Restoration of the papyrus fragment is problematic, but the sense seems clear. Fraenkel (above, note 11) 232–4 contrasts this monologue with the Plautine material. P. W. Harsh, 'The Intriguing Slave in Greek Comedy', *TAPA* 86 (1955) 135–42 adduces other examples. For Habrotonon as a possible intriguing slave see W. G. Arnott, 'Time, Plot and Character in Menander', forthcoming in *Papers of the Liverpool Latin Seminar*, vol. 2 (Liverpool 1979). T. B. L. Webster, *Hellenistic Poetry and Art* (London 1964) 272–3 thinks the prevalence of slave masks in Hellenistic art indicative of the slave's increas-

ing role in drama, but the slender evidence for the fourth and third centuries makes speculation hazardous.

13 A marginal note in the Bodmer papyrus assigns line 383 to Chaireas; Austin give him the concluding lines 387–90 as well. Sandbach, following Gaiser, considers 379 an exit line for Chaireas, and thus gives 383 and 387–90 to Daos. See G–S *ad loc.* OCT's distribution of parts perhaps makes for more effective staging.

14 For Xanthias as a thematic influence in *The Frogs* and ancestor of the clever slaves in subsequent comedy, see K. J. Dover, *Aristophanic Comedy* (Berkeley 1972) 204–8 and Whitman (above, n. 4) 237ff. On the comic power of Pseudolus see J. Wright, 'The Transformations of Pseudolus', *TAPA* 105 (1975) 403–16.

15 A. P. Burnett, *Catastrophe Survived* (Oxford 1971) 81–5 examines in detail Menelaos' inability to play these tragic parts correctly. I am much indebted to her analysis. The characterizations of the *Helen* quoted above are by C. Segal, 'The Two Worlds of Euripides' *Helen*', *TAPA* 102 (1971) 553–614 and C. Wolff, 'On Euripides' *Helen*', *HSCP* 77 (1973) 61–84 respectively.

16 'I shall now', he begins, 'make my speech at your father's tomb, using the *pothos* convention!' (961). His address to Hades revives the old heroic argument for repayment, though his allusion to past deeds of arms is faintly amusing coming from this ragged figure. When the scheme to have him report his own death is suggested, he remarks with obvious truth that the idea is not very original (1056). See Burnett (above, n. 13) 91ff. for discussion of these passages.

CHAPTER IV

1 For the tragedians' originality in plot construction, which is sometimes underrated see H. C. Baldry, 'Aristotle and the Dramatization of Legend', *CQ* 4 (1954) 151–7 and T. B. L. Webster, 'Fourth-Century Tragedy and the *Poetics*', *Hermes* 82 (1954) 294–308. P. E. Legrand, *The Greek New Comedy*, tr. J. Loeb (London 1917) 298–304 discusses the growing importance of plot in post-Aristophanic comedy.

2 A. W. Gomme, 'Menander' in his *Essays in Greek History and Literature* (Oxford 1937) 262. P. M. Levitt, *A Structural Approach to the Analysis of Drama* (The Hague 1971) develops the concept of 'point-of-attack', noting that extensive exposition at the beginning is characteristic of late point-of-attack plays.

3 A. Körte, *Hellenistic Poetry*, tr. J. Hammer and M. Hadas (New York 1929) 32–5 constructed an analogous schema for Menander's fragmentary *Heros* and *Agroikos*, pointing out how the different characterizations of the woman Myrrhine create two apparently distinct courses of action. E. W. Handley, EH 100–2 does something similar with the *Dyskolos* and

Plautus' *Aulularia*. For the plots of *Misoumenos* and *Perikeiromene* see G–S 438–42, 466–9, 511–13.

4 *Poetics* 1449b24. Thus D. W. Lucas, ed., Aristotle, *Poetics* (Oxford 1968) 96: 'It [*praxis*] means, not any random act like opening one's mouth or crossing the street, but an action initiated with a view to an end and carried on in pursuit of it; it can thus include a whole complex of subordinate actions.' See also B. R. Rees, 'Plot, Character and Thought', *Le monde Grec . . . Hommages à Claire Préaux* (Brussels 1975) 188–96. É. Souriau, *Les deux cent mille situations dramatiques* (Paris 1950) 42 observes that 'la situation tout entière est une donnée essentiellement dynamique. Non seulement un système de force en tension intérieure, en arc-boutement; mais encoure un système qui n'est jamais statique . . .'

5 At G–S 505 Sandbach assumed Sosias remains on-stage, a dramatically unnecessary violation of the apparent custom in New Comedy (as in classical tragedy) to have no more than three actors speaking on stage at one time. In his recent article 'Menander and the Three-Actor Rule', *Le Monde Grec* (Brussels 1975) 197–204 Sandbach retracts the suggestion.

6 The very poor state of the papyrus here has obscured the joke about the mill. G–S 481–2 assumes that Daos is asking for a sinecure, and H. Lloyd-Jones, 'Notes on Menander's *Perikeiromene*', *ZPE* 15 (1974) 209–13 cites proverbs to the effect that the miller's life was the good life. Nevertheless, he also offers evidence that Daos' verb μυλωθρεῖν may simply mean 'to work at a mill' rather than 'to run a mill'. Since working at a mill was a favourite punishment for slaves in comedy (cf. *Heros* 3), the humour of this exchange may lie in another direction. A further possibility is a play upon the double sense, Daos asking for a sinecure and Moschion threatening to take him more literally.

7 The new fragment is now available in the *Proceedings of the British Academy* for 1978. I owe special thanks to Professor Turner for making a preliminary transcript available to me. The text translated above is compiled from P. IFAO 89, printed in OCT, and an unnumbered fragment from Oxyrhynchus published by E. G. Turner, *The Papyrologist at Work, GRBM* 6 (Durham, N.C. 1973) 48–50. Line 8 follows an emendation by C. Austin, *ZPE* 13 (1974) 320.

8 P. Oxy. 2826 = 282 Austin; P. Antin. 15 = 240 Austin and OCT, pp. 327–8. For discussions see M. Colantonio, 'Scene notturne nelle commedie di Menandro: nota al P. Oxy. 2826', *QUCC* 23 (1976) 59–66, J. W. B. Barnes and H. Lloyd-Jones, 'A Fragment of New Comedy: P. Antinoopolis 15', *JHS* 84 (1964) 21–34, and T. B. L. Webster, 'Notes on Menander', *Class. et Med. F. Blatt . . . dedicata* (Copenhagen 1973) 137–9.

9 Full text in J. U. Powell, *Collectanea Alexandrina* (Oxford 1925) 177–9. F. O. Copley, *Exclusus Amator: A Study in Latin Love Poetry* (Baltimore 1956) 7–27 discusses the various treatments of the excluded lover theme in Greek literature.

10 The shepherd of Theocritus' *Idyll* 3 mentions the possibility of death repeatedly, and the author of ps.-Theoc. *Idyll* 23 uses the cliché to deft but gruesome effect when *his* lover actually hangs himself from the doorpost. For the motif see F. O. Copley, 'The Suicide Paraclausithyron: A Study in Ps.-Theocritus *Idyll* XXIII', *TAPA* 71 (1940) 52–61.

11 *Moralia* 853e as translated by D. A. Russell in D. A. Russell and M. Winterbottom, *Ancient Literary Criticism* (Oxford 1972) 531. F. H. Sandbach, 'Menander's Manipulation of Language', EH 130–1 remarks on the difficulty of applying this judgement to Menander; he believes this scene in the *Perikeiromene* asks 'rather a lot' of his audience by both using and playing upon tragic conventions (EH 126–8, cf. G–S 519–20).

12 This echo of the *Ion* was noted by W. Kraus, 'Zu Menanders *Misoumenos*', *RhM* 114 (1971) 1–27. G–S 450 discusses the other echoes. *Logos* is used to mean the report of a death at *Aspis* 91 and 161.

13 A. Borgogno, 'Sul *Misoumenos* di Menandro', *SIFC* 41 (1969) 19–55, esp. 24–5 calls attention to this relocation of the recognition scene and its contrast with the *Perikeiromene*. For the normal pattern of recognition comedies see Chapter 5 below.

14 This feature of Terence's technique was noted by the ancient commentators Donatus and Euanthius. See H. Haffter, 'Terenz und seine künstlerische Eigenart', *MH* 10 (1953) 77–9 and especially W. Görler, 'Doppelhandlung, Intrigue und Anagnorismos bei Terenz', *Poetica* 5 (1972) 164–82, who remarks on the rarity of double plots.

CHAPTER V

1 The close relationship between *peripeteia* and *anagnorisis* is emphasized by G. F. Else, *Aristotle's Poetics: The Argument* (Cambridge, Mass. 1957) 342–58. Aristotle's discussion of recognition scenes in this chapter is more basic to an understanding of dramatic *poesis* than the classification of recognitions that follows in Chapter 16, for the impact of a recognition depends more upon its function in the play than on its mechanics. Chapter 14 defines the relationship between *anagnorisis* and tragic action. See H. Phillipart, 'La théorie aristotélicienne de l'anagnorisis', *REG* 38 (1929) 171–204 and D. W. Lucas, 'Pity, Terror and Peripeteia', *CQ* 12 (1962) 56–60.

2 See D. C. Stuart, 'The Function and Dramatic Value of Recognition Scenes in Greek Tragedy', *AJP* 39 (1918) 268–90.

3 'He wrote a comedy called *Kokalos*, in which he introduced rape and recognition and all the other things that Menander emulated,' *Vita Aristophanis* XXVIII. 54–5 in W. J. Koster, ed. *Scholia in Aristophanem I* 1 *a*, *Prolegomena de comoedia* (Groningen 1975) 135. For discussion of the *Kokalos* see G. Murray, *Aristophanes* (Oxford 1933) 208–10.

4 Thus U. von Wilamowitz-Moellendorf, *Das Schiedsgericht* (Berlin 1925) 123: 'Es ist wirklich eine in sich abgerundete Szene, nur lose mit der

Haupthandlung verbunden. Dass die Komödie sich das immer noch erlaubte, ist sehr zu beherzigen.' There may be a deliberate echo of an arbitration scene in Euripides' lost *Alope*, though such a specific antecedent remains only one possibility. The story of Alope as told by Hyginus, *Fabula* 187 includes a similar scene of a grandfather's unknowing judgement over his grandson's tokens, and at least the first part of this story may have constituted the action of Euripides' play. See B. Borecký, 'La tragédie *Alopé* d'Euripide', *Studia Antiqua . . . Antonio Salač* (Prague 1955) 82–9.

5 For discussion of the fragments assigned to Act I see G–S 291–4. Divine prologues in Menander tend to be vague in detail, while expository monologues by human characters are usually heavy with self-characterization. See S. Dworacki, 'The Prologues in the Comedies of Menander', *Eos* 61 (1973) 33–47 and D. Del Corno, 'Prologhi Menandrei', *Acme* 23 (1970) 99–108.

6 κατὰ λογὸν / ἐστὶν βιασμὸν τοῦτον εἶναι παρθένου, 452–3 ('Such an attack on a girl is logical enough') Does Onesimos refer to a genuine 'norm' or simply to a literary convention? Since women were largely segregated in wealthy Athenian society, an encounter at a festival was one of the few opportunities for contact by young people of opposite sexes, but the evidence for such encounters is almost entirely literary (e.g. E. *Ion* 545–4). See K. J. Dover, *Greek Popular Morality in the Time of Plato and Aristotle* (Oxford 1974) 209–13 and W. K. Lacey, *The Family in Classical Greece* (London 1968) 158–62. Penalties for the rape of a free-born Athenian girl could be severe, which may suggest that the events of New Comedy take place in a legal Neverland and that Onesimos' attitude belongs to this fantasy world. It is perhaps noteworthy that Onesimos' *biasmos* is an unusual word for rape; far more common are verbal expressions such as αἰσχύνειν βιᾳ (Lys. 1.32) and ὑβρίζεσθαι βίᾳ (Pl. *Leg.* 847c). Here, as with *anagnorismos* at 1121, Onesimos has chosen an expression more at home in literary discussion, which perhaps indicates a certain artificiality of sentiment. Cf. βιασμοὺς παρθένων in Satyros' life of Euripides (P. Oxy. 1176 fr. 39 col. vii) and παρθένων φθοράς in the ancient biography of Aristophanes cited above, note 3. The difficulty of reconciling the events of New Comedy with our knowledge of Athenian law is discussed by E. Fantham, 'Sex, Status, and Survival in Hellenistic Athens: A Study of Women in New Comedy', *Phoenix* 29 (1975) 46–74.

7 For example χλευάζω and θεῖον for the more common σκώπτω and θαυμάσιον, ἀπολλύει for ἀπόλλυσι (430ff.). For further discussions of Habrotonon's language see S. Zini, *Il linguaggio dei personaggi nelle commedie di Menandro* (Florence 1938) 57–66. F. H. Sandbach, 'Menander's Manipulation of Language', EH 131 notes that the exclamation ὦ θεοί occurs only five times in extant Menander, three of them spoken here by Habrotonon (484, 489, 548). Like her frequent use of ταλάς, they may suggest a further mannerism in her speech.

8 Such flexibility in the use of striking language may be characteristic of the tradition. W. G. Arnott, '*Phormio Parasitus*. A Study in Dramatic Methods of Characterization', *G&R* 17 (1970) 32–57 observes a similar phenomenon in Terence's *Phormio*, which is based upon a Greek original by Apollodoros of Karystos. Flowery language alternates between Geta and Phormio as the play's focus requires. J. Wright, 'The Transformations of Pseudolus', *TAPA* 105 (1975) 403–16 details an analogous manipulation of language in Plautus.

9 The loss of Pamphile's reply unfortunately prevents us from gauging the depth of characterization Menander allotted her. The value of the speech in P. Didot I, which is sometimes cited in this context and is reprinted at OCT 328–30, is, as noted by G–S 357 and 723–4, as a possible parallel for her reply rather than the reply itself. Its relevance, assuming it is indeed a fragment of New Comedy, lies in its evidence for the fact that Pamphile, unlike the silent maids of Terence or Knemon's submissive daughter in the *Dyskolos*, could speak a long, eloquent speech in reply to her father.

10 Thus in proposing arbitration Syriskos uses κριτής (223) and διαλύω (228) for the more technical διαιτητής and διαλάττω, and his ἀντιλέγομεν πρᾶγμά τι (225) is an entirely general expression. J. W. Cohoon, 'Rhetorical Studies in the Arbitration Scene of Menander's *Epitrepontes*', *TAPA* 45 (1914) 141–230 examines the language and construction of these speeches. For the pattern of private arbitrations at Athens see A. R. W. Harrison, *The Laws of Athens*, vol. 2 (Oxford 1971) 64–6.

11 What name did Menander give the charcoal-burner? 'Syriskos' is actually a diminutive of the name Syros and appears only at line 270 of the extant text. The line is faulty on other grounds, and some proposed restorations eliminate the proper name entirely. To complicate things further, the Mytilene mosaic that illustrates this scene calls one character 'Syros' and mislabels his opponent as 'charcoal-burner' (*anthrakeus*). For the textual problem see W. G. Arnott, *CQ* 18 (1968) 227–9 and G–S 309–11. The authority of the mosaic, which is of unknown source and dates from the third century AD, is dubious. We cannot know which form of the name Menander intended, though we may find solace in the realisation that he would probably not think the question crucial. Since no alteration of the line is particularly compelling, we might well accept 'Syriskos' as a *lectio difficilior* and continue to call Daos' rival by that form of the name.

12 This monologue, with the resulting compression of the recognition motif, was apparently Terence's own innovation. The grammarian Aelius Donatus, commenting on the passage in the fourth century AD, remarks that in the Greek original this scene was acted out, not narrated (*ad Hec.* 816 and 825). See K. Büchner, *Das Theater des Terenz* (Heidelberg 1974) 164–7.

13 Terence actually does break the illusion after Bacchis' monologue, something he is not generally inclined to do. Pamphilus' desire to keep the truth from the old men is in effect an appeal for a new ending: 'placet non

fieri hoc itidem ut in comoediis / omnia omnes ubi resciscunt' (866–7). They never learn the true cause of his change of heart in accepting his wife back, a touch of Terentian delicacy well placed to distract attention from the abrupt *ex machina* resolution of the problem. The climactic recognition follows the comic pattern rather mechanically, while the originality of the dénouement is more fresh and appealing. As *anagnorisis* became a familiar and expected part of the tradition, play upon the illusion became more common. At the conclusion of *The Miser* Valère, Anselme and Mariane gaily seek to top each other's version of the saga of Don Thomas d'Alburci, and in Goldoni's *Venetian Twins* Tonino, who has just discovered his twin brother and long lost sister, exclaims, 'Vardè che caso! Vardè che accidente! . . . El par un accidente da commedia!'

14 Else (above, note 1) 353.

CHAPTER VI

1 This vocabulary of misanthropy includes ἀπάνθρωπος and οὐ φιλάνθρωπος, δύσκολος, ἐρημία, μόνος and μονοτρόπος, οὐ χαίρων ὄχλῳ and μισοπονήρος. For the type see W. Schmid, 'Menanders *Dyskolos* und die Timonlegende', *RhM* 102 (1959) 157–82 and W. Görler, 'Knemon', *Hermes* 91 (1963) 268–87. The *Dyskolos* itself influenced the later tradition, as evidenced by Aelian's *Rustic Letters* 13–16 and Lucian's dialogue *Timon* in the second century AD. For these developments see P. Photiades 'Le type du misanthrope dans la littérature grecque', *CE* 68 (1959) 305–26, and I. L. Thyresson, 'Quatre lettres de Claude Elien inspirées par le Dyscolos de Ménandre', *Eranos* 62 (1964) 7–25.

2 Well discussed by C. Préaux, 'La misanthrope au théâtre', *CE* 68 (1959) 327–41.

3 The influence of Pan on the ensuing action is best discussed by A. Pastorino, 'Aspetti religioso del *Dyscolos* di Menandro', *Menandrea* (Genoa 1960) 79–106 and W. Ludwig, 'Die *Cistellaria* und das Verhältnis von Gott und Handlung bei Menander', *EH* 84–91. For Pan's language in the prologue and its thematic significance see S. M. Goldberg, 'The Style and Function of Menander's *Dyskolos* Prologue', *SO* 53 (1978) 57–68.

4 Similar questions to elicit expository information are posed in Menander's *Heros* 4–5 and *Aspis* 19, cf. Terence *HT* 61–2 and *Eun.* 46. In the opening scene of *Pseudolus* Plautus plays upon the conventional device by having Pseudolus expand on the very need to ask the question. E. Fraenkel, *Elementi plautini in Plauto* (Florence 1960) 390–3 contrasts this Plautine embellishment with the *Heros* fragment. The expository function of the dialogue with Chaireas and Pyrrhias is well analyzed by A. Schäfer, *Menanders Dyskolos* (Meisenheim 1965) 34–41, hereafter cited in this chapter as *Schäfer*.

5 E. W. Handley, *The Dyskolos of Menanders* (London 1965) 143, hereafter cited in this chapter as *Handley*, offers the entrance of Amphitheos at

Acharnians 176ff. as a prototype. Other examples are more speculative. The two lines of Menander, fr. 690 K–T may suggest a running messenger. Another possible candidate is P. Hibeh 5 fr. a, reprinted at OCT 338. On these passages see T. Guardì, 'I precedenti greci della figura del servus currens della commedia romana', *Pan* 2 (1974) 5–15, which errs, however, in identifying Daos of *Aspis* 399ff. as another example. For the Roman *servus currens* see G. Duckworth, *The Nature of Roman Comedy* (Princeton 1952) 106–7. For Chaireas as parasite or fawner see *Handley* 140–41. Note how the repeated taus and omegas of his opening lines help make the speech a set piece.

6 Does Pyrrhias re-enter at 214? This is the intention of the papyrus, which has a dicolon after *kakodaimon*, a paragraphos, and the note 'Pyrrhias' in the right margin. *Handley* 27 therefore suggests that he has overheard Sostratos at 181, perhaps shown to the audience as an extra in costume and mask by the door of the shrine. This is the most plausible interpretation of such punctuation, but it is open to two serious objections. First, there would have to be an extremely quick change of costume for the actor playing the girl and Pyrrhias, even granting Handley's point that 217 is spoken from within the door. Second, there is no dramatic need to reintroduce Pyrrhias, either seen at 181, where his appearance might distract attention from Sostratos' monologue, or heard at 214, where he would be a pointless intrusion between Sostratos' speech and Daos' reaction to it. The correct explanation, accepted by G–S 170, was made independently by E. Grassi, 'Note a Menandro', *A&R* 6 (1961) 144 and T. B. L. Webster, 'Self-Apostrophe in Menander', *CR* 15 (1965) 17–18. Lines 213–17 are spoken by Sostratos himself, interrupted by Daos' aside. Similar self-apostrophes are found at *Epitr.* 913ff. and probably 979ff. and at *Dis Ex.* 23ff. The punctuation and marginal note in the papyrus either arose through misunderstanding of the passage, or the dicolon may originally have been intended to mark the change of tone in the monologue and was then misinterpreted and the paragraphos added. If this interpretation is correct, is Pyrrhias' disappearance at 144 unmotivated? Hardly, for Knemon's appearance is ample reason for any right-thinking person to vanish, as Chaireas does. Pyrrhias' entire scene is one of flight. He is eager to get away. The motion of the act is toward exits, first Chaireas, then Pyrrhias, and then, having failed to approach Knemon, Sostratos. To bring Pyrrhias back for a gratuitous few lines runs contrary to the flow of action.

7 Aristotle, *EN* 1112a, cf. 1103a31ff. This psychology is particularly suited to drama, for it allows the dramatist to demonstrate character through action, the method most appropriate to his medium. Thus Aristotle emphasizes that drama represents men in action, and he sees choice (*proairesis*) as a key element in dramatizing character. See *Poetics* 1448a1 and 1450b8ff. M. Anderson, 'Knemon's *hamartia*', *G&R* 17 (1970) 199–207 develops the point in the context of the *Dyskolos*.

8 For the parallels see *Handley* 158. The closest is perhaps Menander, fr. 718K–T (OCT 321) where the mythological example is also unexpectedly twisted, this time by pinning Prometheus to his rock for having created woman.

9 *Handley* 164–5 likens the lamenting girl with her water jar to Euripides' Electra and cites as parallels for the tragic diction Aeschylus, *Pers.* 445 and Euripides, *Phoen.* 373. E. G. Turner, EH 27 thinks the echo of Electra 'a fairly recondite allusion'; what is significant is the way Menander builds upon a complex of echoes, verbal and probably visual, that would clearly be recognized as tragic, though only some in the audience might be able to cite a particular tragic prototype.

10 The text of this exchange is in some doubt; the papyrus may indicate a change of speaker at 196. There is a dicolon but no paragraphos, perhaps intending to mark a break in the speech rather than a change of speaker. If the rest of the line is given to Sostratos, another oath is the likely restoration. See *Handley* 166 and G–S 167. P. Flury, *Liebe und Liebessprache bei Menander, Plautus und Terenz* (Heidelberg 1968) 38 detects 'a paratragic ring' in Sostratos' exclamation intended to make his position amusing without being laughable. The suddenness of the girl's appearance and the social barriers ordinarily imposed between young men and women of Sostratos' class might help rationalize his incoherence, but the volubility of his oaths is surely intended to make his position comic, if not slightly foolish.

11 The technique of introducing a new development just before an act break was first discussed by E. W. Handley, 'The Conventions of the Comic Stage', EH 11–13 and the discussion at 27–9. For the social tension in the play see E. S. Ramage, 'City and Country in Menander's *Dyskolos*', *Philologus* 110 (1966) 194–211 and D. Del Corno, 'Il problema dell' urbanesimo in Menandro', *Dioniso* 43 (1969) 85–94.

12 The scene is discussed well by W. G. Arnott, 'The Confrontation of Sostratos and Gorgias', *Phoenix* 18 (1964) 110–123 and F. H. Sandbach, 'Menander's Manipulation of Language', EH 116–19. It may be noted that the formality of Gorgias' speech here is primarily a device for heightening the contrast between them and is not an indelible mark of his character. As noted by *Handley* 176, his address to Daos at 234ff. is much less rigid. Distinctive language is used only as the dramatic situation requires, much as was done with Habrotonon in the *Epitrepontes*. W. Görler, 'Menander, *Dyskolos* 233–381 und Terenz, *Eunuchus* 817–922', *Philologus* 105 (1961) 299–307 observes striking similarities of structure between these two scenes which may suggest a formulaic type of confrontation that depends upon elaborate characterisations for its individuality.

13 Compare Gorgias' parallel negatives at 324–5 and 329–31 with Pan's emphatic negatives at 10 and, for example, Phrynichos fr. 18K, the *Monotropos* fragment quoted above. For Gorgias' 'how sweet to one . . .' compare the *Hydria* fragment. Note the emphatic position of the key word

monos at 329 and 331; Sostratos uses *chalepos* at 325, a twin of the key word *dyskolos* (cf. 628, 747).

14 See for example L. A. Post, 'Virtue Promoted in Menander's *Dyscolus*', *TAPA* 91 (1960) 152–61 and B.A. van Groningen, 'The Delineation of Character in Menander's *Dyscolus*,' *Recherches de Papyrologie* 1 (1961) 95–112. *Schäfer* 29–30 argued that while Knemon is intended to be a central figure, the main interest lies with Sostratos and the play is really a *Liebesromanze*. This led him to examine what he called 'the disintegration of a double plot' (75ff.), and he concluded that the crucial problem with the *Dyskolos* is Menander's failure to combine these two elements successfully. Viewing the play as a series of situations all linked by the device of approaching the *dyskolos* may help overcome Schäfer's objection.

15 The attribution of parts here is in some doubt, though the lively intention of the scene is clear. OCT is probably correct to give a speaking part to Sostratos' mother. See G–S 200–3 and, for arguments on the other side, *Handley* 207–9. In favour of OCT are the usually feminine exclamation *talan* at 438 and the lack of precedent in Greek drama for the entry of a party without a speaker among them. Three speakers are universally accepted for the scene. *Handley* introduced Sikon at 434. Use of the expression 'to us' at 437 is not really appropriate to him, however, since strictly speaking he is working for the party rather than being part of it. Note Getas' 'to you' at 555. Further, while there is no dramatic gain in introducing the cook, use of the mother to animate the approaching party makes Knemon's complaint about the crowd at 431 more appropriate and provides a better motivation for the action.

16 H. Dohm, *Mageiros* (Munich 1964) 243 notes Menander's restriction of the cook's normal loquacity, while *Handley* 220 observes the similarity of form with Chaireas' monologue at 57ff. Contrast the more typical expansion of the cook's speech in Alexis' *Cauldron* (*Lebes*, fr. 127K) and *The Night Festival* (*Pannychis* fr. 174K).

17 This similarity of structure was noted by T. B. L. Webster, *Studies in Menander*, 2 ed. (Manchester 1960) 229. Some have questioned the existence of the *ekkyklema* to show internal scenes at this time, but both *Handley* 263–4 and G–S 239–41 adopt the commonsense view that *some* device, probably wheeled, is parodied by Aristophanes and used here by Menander as a tragic echo. For what it is worth, the highly probable restoration εἰσκυ]κλεῖτ' at 758 is the *vox propria* for the withdrawal of the *ekkyklema* (cf. Pollux, *Onomastikon* iv. 128). The device itself and the argument for its existence in classical times is discussed by P. Arnott, *Greek Scenic Conventions in the Fifth Century B.C.* (Oxford 1962) 78–88.

18 T. Drew-Bear, 'The Trochaic Tetrameter in Greek Tragedy', *AJP* 89 (1968) 385–405 observes this use of the metre in the *Agamemnon, Oedipus, Philoctetes, Helen*, and *Iphigenia at Aulis*. Also M. Imhof, 'Tetrameterszene in der Tragödie', *MH* 13 (1956) 125–43. This tragic usage tells against the suggestion of F. Perusino, 'Tecnica e stile nel tetrametro trocaico di

Menandro', *RCCM 4* (1962) 45–64 that the seriousness of Knemon's speech is undercut by the rhythm.

19 Contrast the comparative disorder of Gorgias' lines with the formulaic language of comic betrothal used by Kallipides at 842ff. (cf. *Mis.* 444ff., *Perik.* 1013ff. and G–S 531 for further examples). The only formal language we know for Athenian betrothals comes from comic passages such as these. See A. R. W. Harrison, *The Laws of Athens*, vol. 1 (Oxford 1968) 3–9 on betrothals and 48–54 on dowries.

20 The relationship of this scene to the rest of the play is treated especially well by *Schäfer* 63–6.

CHAPTER VII

1 F. Stoessl, 'Unkenntnis und Missverstehen als Prinzip und Quelle der Komik in Menanders *Samia*', *RhM* 116 (1973) 21–45 observes that the comedy is built around the process of getting the necessary information to the right people. It is important to remember, though, that Moschion can resolve the dilemma at a stroke simply by telling the truth to Demeas. His moral cowardice both initiates and prolongs the action. Glykera of the *Perikeiromene* might seem to be in a similar position, since she knows Moschion is her brother and could resolve the crisis by telling Polemon. The soldier's behaviour, however, has given her understandable cause to keep silent. Moschion of the *Samia* has no such excuse.

2 See F. Wehrli, *Motivstudien zur griechischen Komödie* (Zurich & Leipzig 1936) 56–69. P. E. Legrand, *The New Greek Comedy*, tr. J. Loeb (London & New York 1917) 129–38 bases his survey on the Latin adaptations of the theme.

3 For the moral colouring of Moschion's language and its influence on the action see H. J. Mette, 'Moschion ὁ κόσμος', *Hermes* 97 (1969) 432–9 and M. Treu, 'Humane Handlungsmotive in der *Samia* Menanders', *RhM* 112 (1969) 230–54. D. Del Corno, 'Prologhi Menandrei', *Acme* 23 (1970) 99–108 contrasts his speech with the other extant Menandrean prologues.

4 H.-D. Blume, *Menanders Samia, eine Interpretation* (Darmstadt 1974) 12–15, hereafter cited as *Blume*, observes the irony of Moschion's self-assured judgement of another love affair. Though both Mette (above, note 3) and F. Stoessl, 'Die neuen Menanderpublikationen der Bibliotheca Bodmeriana in Genf', *RhM* 112 (1969) 193–229, p. 196 believe that Moschion played an active part in bringing Demeas and Chrysis together, nothing in Demeas' own speeches or actions suggests reticence on his part, nor does he ever confirm the truth of Moschion's account.

5 *Blume* 33 rightly calls attention to the visual impact of their entrance, suggesting a contrast between the wealthy Demeas directing his porters and Nikeratos, certainly dressed more plainly and perhaps carrying his own belongings. Such an arrival may have been a *topos* of New Comedy.

See *Blume* 36–7 and J. Wright, *Dancing in Chains* (Rome 1974) 141–51, who discusses its expansion for comic effect by Plautus.

6 Nikeratos' complaint about the wormwood and fish is echoed in Diphilos, fr. 17K, where a cook is explaining how to treat various foreigners:

> If they're Byzantines,
> serve up a dish with wormwood ground in,
> and make everything full of salt and garlic.
> That's because of all the fish among them.

They're all clammy and thoroughly phlegmatic.

Menander, fr. 61K–T complains of their drinking habits. It is Sandbach, not the Bodmer papyrus, who gives lines 98–101 to Nikeratos, but his arguments are persuasive. See EH 120–1, endorsed by E. G. Turner, EH 138–9 and T. B. L. Webster, *CW* 64 (1970) 238. *Blume* 33–47 prefers the manuscript punctuation, which gives 96–105 all to Demeas; he interprets the contrast between Byzantion and Athens much more seriously.

7 Chrysis was Demeas' *pallake*, a common-law wife, and her social position at Athens, even if she was free, was tenuous. See E. W. Bushala, 'The *Pallake* of Philoneus', *AJP* 90 (1969) 65–72 and A. R. W. Harrison, *The Laws of Athens*, vol 1 (Oxford 1968) 13–15. The terms *hetaira* and *pallake* are used interchangeably of Chrysis (21, 25, 130; 508). Cf. Ps.-Demosthenes 59.118, where Neaira is called *hetaira* and *pallake* in successive sentences.

8 D. B. Thompson, 'The Origin of Tanagras', *AJA* 70 (1966) 51–63 illustrates the popularity of such figurines and draws the parallel with this passage. Talkative old ladies were frequent targets of Attic comedy; the old lady Parmenon later orders kept away from the wine jars is often identified with this nurse (302–3 and G–S *ad loc.*). For the type see H. G. Oeri, *Der Typ der komischen Alten in der griechischen Komödie* (Basel 1948) 12–18, 38–46.

9 Direct address to the audience with this vocative is used four times by Demeas (269, 329, 447, 734), only once by Moschion (683). The significance of Demeas' frequent address can be illustrated by comparison with the *Dyskolos*. There, in a text some two hundred lines longer, the vocative is used only four times, by Sostratos (194, 666), Sikon (659), and Getas (967). For general discussion of the device see D. Bain, *Actors and Audience* (Oxford 1977) 190–94 and G–S 14–15.

10 See W. G. Arnott, 'A Note on the Motif of "Eavesdropping Behind the Door" in Comedy', *RhM* 108 (1965) 371–6 and *Blume* 86–7.

11 G–S 618 identifies the tragic echoes and incongruities in Moschion's speech; W. S. Anderson, 'The Ending of the *Samia* and other Menandrian Comedies', *Studi classici in onore di Q. Cataudella*, vol. 2 (Catania 1972) 155–79 remarks on his absurdity. Menander's Moschions tend to be weak, often distasteful characters. This Moschion is more fully portrayed and consequently more likeable than most. The worst of the lot may be Moschion of the *Sikyonios*, whom the messenger describes as effeminate and dandified in contrast with someone manly, probably the 'hero'

Stratophanes. See W. T. MacCary, 'Menander's Characters', *TAPA* 101 (1970) 277–90, esp. 286–9.

12 Thus in the dining room of the House of Menander at Mytilene, where the mosaics illustrate one significant scene from each of a variety of plays, Chrysis' expulsion in Act III was chosen to represent the *Samia*. See S. Charitonidis, L. Kahil & R. Ginouvès, *Les Mosaïques de la Maison du Ménandre à Mytilène, Antike Kunst Beiheft* 6 (Bern 1970) for full discussion. A. Barigazzi, *Il formazione spirituale di Menandro* (Turin 1965) 176–80 and 'Sulla nuova e vecchio *Samia* di Menandro', *RFIC* 98 (1970) 156–8 emphasizes those aspects of Chrysis' *nobilità* implied by the text.

13 E. Keuls 'The *Samia* of Menander, an Interpretation of its Plot and Theme', *ZPE* 10 (1973) 1–20 fails in an attempt to claim Chrysis as the subject of a genuine sub-plot. The truth is put bluntly by E. Fantham, 'Sex, Status, and Survival in Hellenistic Athens: A Study of Women in New Comedy', *Phoenix* 29 (1975) 44–74: 'For the dramatist it would seem her problems and her honour were of no more concern; his real interest is the man-to-man relationship of Demeas and his adopted son, and Chrysis once back in the household is forgotten' (66).

14 Attempts to reconstruct lost or fragmentary plays often founder on Menander's highly selective choice of details to build upon. Before the rest of the *Samia* was published in 1969, for example, some scholars hypothesized an ending in which Chrysis was found to be Moschion's sister and married Demeas. For the measure of past conjecture against the new text see H. Lloyd-Jones, 'Menander's *Samia* in the Light of the New Evidence', *YCS* 22 (1972) 119–44. U. von Wilamowitz-Moellendorf, 'Die *Samia* des Menanders', an article first published in 1916 and reprinted in his *Kleine Schriften* I (Berlin 1935) 415–39 was among the few early critics to appreciate Menander's refusal to give equal value to all details and moods in a play. As he observed of the first expulsion scene, 'angelegt ist die ganze Szene auf Demeas; Chrysis ist Folie' (429).

CHAPTER VIII

1 J. Wright, *Dancing in Chains* (Rome 1974) 138–51 identifies four elements in the Latin arrival scene: entrance with porters, prayer of thanksgiving for safe arrival, greeting from friend who invites traveller to dinner, exit into house. We find the traveller's address to his homeland in Menander, fr. 1K–T, fr. 287K–T, *Aspis* 491, and perhaps Kock's Adesp. fr. 340. E. W. Handley restores the beginning of a similar address in the *Phasma*, P. Oxy. 2825 fr. C (not in OCT): Ἀπολλον ὦ π]άροικ' ἄναξ after *Bacchides* 172: saluto te, vicine Apollo . . . For discussion of the parallel texts of *Dis Exapaton* and *Bacchides* see E. W. Handley, *Menander and Plautus: A Study in Comparison* (London 1968), K. Gaiser, 'Die plautinischen *Bacchides* und Menanders *Dis Exapaton*', *Philologus* 114 (1970) 51–87, D. Del Corno, 'Alcuni aspetti del linguaggio di Menandro', *SCO* 24 (1975)

13–48, and E. Lefèvre, 'Plautus Studien II,' *Hermes* 106 (1978) 518–538.

2 For the stage setting of New Comedy and the techniques for its expansion see T. B. L. Webster, 'Menander: Production and Imagination', *Bull. J. Rylands Library* 45 (1962/63) 235–72. Also see his *Greek Theatre Production* (London 1956) 22–8, E. W. Handley, 'The Conventions of the Comic Stage', EH 18–23, and G. Duckworth, *The Nature of Roman Comedy* (Princeton 1952) 121–7.

3 A similar off-stage event probably initiated the action of Menander's *Phasma*, for which see E. G. Turner, 'The *Phasma* of Menander', *GRBS* 10 (1969) 307–24. Such a passage between the common wall of adjoining houses is not entirely far-fetched. Turner cites P. Oxy. 1607, which refers to an actual scandal in Menander's boyhood arising from just such a ploy.

4 Thraso's 'lepu' tute's, pulpamentum quaeris?' ('You're a hare and you go after game?' *Eun.* 446) probably goes back to Livius Andronicus, traditional founder of the *palliata*. A Greek proverb of similar sentiment may have stood in Terence's original (apparently Menander's *Kolax*), but the Latin expansion is clearly intended to be as familiar to the audience as to the parasite Gnatho. For the history of the joke see Wright (above, note 1) 24–7. A Roman origin for military boasts of the kind found at *Curc.* 439ff. and *MG* 38ff. is suggested by J. A. Hanson, 'The Glorious Military', *Roman Drama*, ed. T. A. Dorey & D. R. Dudley (London 1965) 56–8.

5 G. F. Else, *Aristotle's Poetics: The Argument* (Cambridge, Mass. 1957) 320, commenting on *Poetics* 1451b27–32. Cf. T. S. Eliot, 'Tradition and the Individual Talent', *The Sacred Wood* (London 1934) 58 [= *Selected Essays* (London & New York 1950) 10]: 'The business of the poet is not to find new emotions, but to use the ordinary ones and, in working them up into poetry, to express feelings which are not in actual emotions at all.'

6 For the difficulty of revealing internal thought and responses to that difficulty, see U. Ellis-Fermor, *The Frontiers of Drama* (London 1964) 96ff.

7 C. Price, *Theatre in the Age of Garrick* (Oxford 1973) 6–42 discusses the acting techniques of Garrick and his contemporaries in detail.

8 E. W. Handley, *The Dyskolos of Menander* (London 1965) 27–30. N. C. Hourmouziades, 'Menander's Actors', *GRBS* 14 (1973) 179–88 is unhappy with the need to divide roles among actors but can offer no plausible alternative. Also see F. H. Sandbach, 'Menander and the Three-Actor Rule', *Le Monde Grec . . . Hommages à Claire Préaux* (Brussels 1975) 197–204. For ancient acting techniques see A. W. Pickard-Cambridge, *The Dramatic Festivals of Athens*, 2 ed. (Oxford 1968) 167–76, A. M. Dale, 'The Creation of Dramatic Characters', *Collected Papers* (Cambridge 1969) 272–80, and P. Walcot, *Greek Drama in its Theatrical and Social Context* (Cardiff 1976) 44–75.

9 Philostr. *VA* 2.22 as translated by F. C. Conybeare in the Loeb Philostratos, *The Life of Apollonius of Tyana*, vol. 1 (London & New York 1912) 173–9. At 6.19 Philostratos is led to distinguish between *mimesis* as copy-

ing and free creation, which he calls *phantasia*. A fine discussion of Philostratos' concept of *mimesis* is in E. H. Gombrich, *Art and Illusion* (New York 1960) 181–202. The origin of the ideas in the *Life* is shadowy. Apollonios was a neo-Pythagorean sage of the first century AD and Philostratos a scholar born in the late second. See G. W. Bowersock, *Greek Sophists in the Roman Empire* (Oxford 1969) 1–16 and W. Schmid-O. Stählin, *Geschichte der griechischen Literatur*, vol. 2 pt. 2 (Munich 1924) 776–7.

10 The scholarly literature is immense. See G. F. Else, ' "Imitation" in the Fifth Century,' *CP* 53 (1958) 73–90, G. Sörbom, *Mimesis and Art* (Uppsala 1966), and the appendix to D. W. Lucas' edition of the *Poetics* (Oxford 1968) 258–72. The link between Aristophanes' epigram and Aristotelian literary theory is emphasized by R. Cantarella, 'Aristofane di Bisanzio, Menandro e la mimesi', *RAL* 24 (1969) 189–94 = *Scritti minori sul teatro greco* (Brescia 1970) 443–8.

11 Gombrich (above, note 9) 141. The interplay of creation and perception in art is the main theme of *Art and Illusion*, and readers of that book will at once recognize how much this discussion owes to it. The story of Socrates and Parrhasios is in Xenophon, *Memorabilia* 3.10.

12 Or perhaps Menander's; we cannot tell how closely Terence followed his original here. For what it is worth, Donatus remarks on *Andria* 891: 'mira gravitate sensus elatus est; nec de Menandro, sed proprium Terentii.' That Terence could alter the *dianoia* of a scene is suggested by Micio's behaviour at the end of *The Brothers*, of which Donatus says, 'apud Menandrum senex de nuptiis non gravatur; ergo Terentius εὑρετικῶς' (ad *Ad.* 938). The actual changes Terence made have long been a matter of controversy. Two recent discussions are J. N. Grant, 'The Ending of Terence's *Adelphoe* and the Menandrian Original', *AJP* 96 (1975) 42–60 and C. Lord, 'Aristotle, Menander and the *Adelphoe*', *TAPA* 107 (1977) 183–202. For Aristotle's concept of *dianoia* see Else (above, note 5) 263ff.

13 The basic sense of ἀπό is of separation commonly in the concrete sense of *spatial displacement* e.g. ἀποβαίνω and ἀποδίδομι. It can also suggest something transferred in the abstract, especially in middle forms, e.g. ἀποκρίνομαι and ἀποδέχομαι. See P. Chantraine, *Dictionnaire étymologique de la langue grecque* (Paris 1968) s.v. ἀπό. The compound ἀπομιμέομαι, as distinct from the simple verb, perhaps emphasises that something is actually captured and moved from the original to the new creation. Compare ἀπόμάττειν, 'to take an impression', at *Frogs* 1040 and Philostr. *VA* 6.19.

14 Probably a very keen eye. Aristophanes apparently wrote a treatise on plagiarisms in Menander, which certainly indicates that he paid close attention to Menander's use of language. See P. M. Fraser, *Ptolemaic Alexandria*, vol. 2 (Oxford 1972) 1055 n. 271. Whether this work was a philological study of Menandrean usage, perhaps motivated by Aristophanes' admiration for Menander, or an Alexandrian polemic remains, *pace* Fraser, a moot question. For Aristophanes' career as a scholar see

Fraser, vol. 1, 459–61; for his love of Menander, R. Pfeiffer, *History of Classical Scholarship* vol. 1 (Oxford 1968) 190–2.

15 Else (above, note 5) 256–7. Cf. Ellis-Fermor (above, note 6) 7: 'One of the actual limitations of drama against which the greatest dramatists have often chafed is its refusal to display the multifariousness of life.'

16 For Theophrastos' definition of comedy see A. Plebe, *La teoria del comico da Aristotele a Plutarco* (Turin 1952) 43–6. The scholion on Dionysios Thrax is XVIII.B.1 in W. J. W. Koster, *Scholia in Aristophanem I* 1a, *Prolegomena de comoedia* (Groningen 1975). Donatus, *de comoedia* V.1 = XXVI Koster. This critical language is full of clichés, and Cicero's piling up of phrases is also characteristic of the Greek definitions. Compare the language of XIb Koster, an anonymous treatise on comedy.

17 This point is developed by C. Préaux, 'Ménandre et la société athénienne', *CE* 63 (1957) 84–100, who observes: '. . . il nous faut rappeler que la comédie n'a pas pour fonction de nous peindre la vie même, mais de nous venger de notre impuissance à la faire comme nous la voudrions.'

18 J. P. Eckermann, *Gespräche mit Goethe in den letzen Jahren seines Leben* for 12 May 1825. The context was Menander, of whom Goethe spoke warmly: 'Nächst dem Sophokles kennen ich keinen, der mir so liebe wäre. Er ist durchaus rein, edel, gross und heiter; seine Anmut ist unerreichbar.'

Index

(Figures in brackets refer to notes)

Act structure, 14, 78, 137 (11), 140 (11)

Acting styles, 6, 113–14, 142 (8)

Aelian, 135 (1)

Aeschylus, *Eumenides*, 6; *Libation Bearers*, 26, 60; *Persians*, 36

Alexandrian Erotic Fragment, An, 52

Alexis, 9, 138 (16); fr. 90K, 5; fr. 142K, 32

Alkaios, 127 (9)

Anaxandrides, fr. 17K, 5; fr. 39K, 35

Antiphanes, 9, 32, 72; fr. 166K, 5; fr. 191K, 112; fr. 221K, 5; fr. 231K, 7

Apollodoros, 128 (8)

Apollonios of Tyana, 116–17, 142 (9)

Arbitration, dramatized, 66–8, 132 (4); in law, 134 (10)

Aristophanes, parody of tragedy, 16–17, 26, 31, 60; plot in, 24, 44; recognition scenes in, 60; *Acharnians*, 2, 3, 4, 16–17, 23, 30, 136 (5); *Birds*, 2, 3, 4, 26, 32; *Clouds*, 2, 26, 93; *Frogs*, 3, 18, 19, 41, 111; *Knights*, 60; *Kokalos*, 60; *Peace*, 4, 8; *Thesmophoriazusae*, 31; *Wasps*, 2, 93; *Wealth*, 2–4, 9, 13

Aristophanes of Byzantion, 109, 112, 117, 119–20, 143 (14)

Aristotle, 7, 14, 117; *dianoia* in, 118; on dramatic character, 75, 112, 120, 136 (7); on maxims, 88; on plot, 44, 47, 57; on recognitions, 59–60, 71

Audience, address to, 98, 102, 106, 111, 140 (9); expectations of, 21, 27, 67, 75, 114; liveliness of, 5, 6; response of, 8–9, 113, 116, 121

Axionikos, 16

Betrothal formula, 87, 106, 139 (19)

Bios, in drama, 4, 14, 112, 120

Birth tokens, 53–4, 60, 66, 67, 68

Books, ancient, 11–12

Burnett, A. P., 17, 130 (15), 130 (16)

Byzantines, in comedy, 140 (6)

Chorus, 3, 14

Cicero, 120

Comedy, changes in after Aristophanes, 4–5; domestic interest of, 2, 14, 114, 116, 121; excluded lover in, 51; plot in, 24, 44

Comoedia palliata, 9, 12, 19, 112, 142 (4)

Commedia dell' arte, 12

Cook, *see* Stock characters

Death, in comedy, 29, 30–1, 33, 36, 51, 52

Demosthenes, 6

Dianoia, 118, 143 (12)

Dio Chrysostom, 12

Diomedes, grammarian, 120

Dionysios Thrax, 120

Diphilos, 9; fr. 17K, 140 (6); fr. 60K, 16; fr. 73K, 15, 19, 22, 30

Doctor, *see* Stock characters

Donatus, 120, 132, (14), 134 (12), 143 (12)

Double plot, 56–7, 106–7, 138 (14), 141 (13)

Dramatic illusion, 27–8, 70, 74, 89, 134 (13)
Dramatic situation, 24, 47, 57–8, 107, 127 (7)

Eavesdropping, 99, 140 (10)
Editor, task of, 10, 12
Ekkyklema, 16, 18, 85, 138 (17)
Eliot, T. S., 2, 142 (5)
Else, G., 71, 112, 120, 132 (1), 143 (10)
Entrance line, 17–18, 75, 135 (4)
Epicharmos, 128 (5)
Epidikasia, 129 (9)
Euripides, as comic butt, 15–17; echoes of, 54–5; model for innovation, 17, 26, 43; *Alope*, 18, 132 (4); *Auge*, 30, 70; *Electra*, 18, 77; *Helen*, 26, 41–3, 60; *Herakles*, 85; *Hippolytos*, 83, 99; *Ion*, 55, 59, 60, 61, 67, 69; *Iphigenia at Tauris*, 15, 60; *Kresphontes*, 6; *Orestes*, 6, 23, 127 (9)
Exangelos, 31, 33, 40, 83, 87, 99

Farce, 32, 48–50, 83, 89–90, 103–4
Foreigner, *see* Stock characters
Fraenkel, E., 128 (5), 129 (11, 12), 135 (4)
Frye, N., 127 (8), 128 (1)

Garrick, D., 114
Gatekeeper scene, 25–7, 41
Goethe, J. W. von, 121, 144 (18)
Goldoni, C., 12, 29, 30, 135 (13)
Gombrich, E. H., 118, 143 (9)
Gomme, A. W., 45, 127 (10)

Hegelochos, actor, 6

Jachmann, G., v

Kallipides, actor, 6
Katsouris, A. G., 127 (9), 129 (10)

Kyrieia, 37, 66

Law, Athenian, 128 (3), 129 (9), 133 (6), 134 (10), 140 (7)

Masks, 13, 33, 44, 52, 114, 126 (1), 129 (12)
Menander, characterizing diction, 63, 79, 80, 103, 133 (7), 137 (12); discovery of papyri, 9, 13; distribution of roles, 20–1; double plot, 57, 106–7, 138 (14); gatekeeper scenes, 26–7; life of, 9, 13; problem of reconstruction, 141 (14); signs of tradition in, 13–14, 44–5; tragic echoes, 23–4, 27, 30, 33, 37, 54–5, 83, 85–6, 100; *Dis Exapaton*, 109, 136 (6), 141 (1); *Heros*, 61, 130 (3), 131 (6), 135 (4); *Kolax*, 45, 111; *Misoumenos*, Chapter 4, passim; *Perinthia*, 25, 39, 40; *Phasma*, 141 (1), 142 (3); *Sikyonios*, 10, 12, 13, 22–3, 76, 98, 127, (9), 140 (11); fr. 1K-T, 141 (1); fr. 11K-T, 72; fr. 61K-T, 140 (6); fr. 287K-T, 141 (1); fr. 401K-T, 73, 137 (13); fr. 554K-T, 45; fr. 598K-T, 94; fr. 690K-T, 136 (5); fr. 718K-T, 137 (8); fr. 745K-T, 45; fr. 794–5K-T, 129 (8); fr. 805K-T, 129 (8)
Metre, distinctions between tragic and comic, 7–8, 19; effect of change in, 86, 89, 104, 138 (18); tragic (in Aristophanes) 8, 60, (in Menander) 54–5
Mimesis, 116–19
Misanthrope, *see* Stock characters
Miser, *see* Stock characters
Modes, defined, 22
Molière, 112, *Misanthrope*, 73, 86; *Miser*, 12, 61, 68, 135 (13)
Mytilene mosaics, 114, 134 (11), 141 (12)

New Comedy, v, 19, 44, 111, 112, 114, 121
Nietzsche, F., v
Nikolaos, 35

Obscenity, 3, 48
O'Keeffe, J., 19
Old Comedy, 3, 30, 109, 125 (1)
Old Woman, see Stock characters
Oratio recta, in monologues, 12, 64, 76, 84, 98

P. Antinoopolis 15, 51
P. Didot I, 134 (9)
P. Hibeh 5 fr. a, 136 (5)
P. Oxy. 11, 39
P. Oxy. 1607, 142 (3)
P. Oxy. 2659, 128 (5)
P. Oxy., 2826, 51, 131 (8)
Pallake, 140 (7)
Papyrus, 10
Paraclausithyron, 52
Parasite, see Stock characters
Parmenon, actor, 6
Parody, 7, 30, 127 (9); Aristophanic, 16, 31, 60; audience response to, 20, 31
Parrhasios, painter, 118–19
Pherekrates, 72
Philippides, 16
Philostratos, 116–17, 143 (13)
Phrygians, in comedy, 35, 36, 128 (8)
Phrynichos, 72, 137 (13)
Plato, 117, 118
Plautus, 1, 9, 12, 19, 93; traveller motif in, 109–10; *Amphitruo*, 120; *Bacchides*, 9, 39, 109, 141 (1); *Mercator*, 51; *Miles Gloriosus*, 38–9, 110; *Pseudolus*, 39, 41, 134 (8), 135 (4); *Rudens*, 67–8; *Truculentus*, 93, 111
Plutarch, 6, 9, 44, 54
Point-of-attack, 45, 130 (2)
Point of view, 21
Pollux, Julius, 126 (1), 138 (17)

Porson's bridge, 8, 19
Prologues, 8, 45, 54, 62, 92, 95, 133 (5); *Aspis*, 34, 37; *Dyskolos*, 74–5, 80; *Samia*, 92–3
Proverbs, 88, 128 (8), 131 (6)
Punctuation, problems of, 11–12, 130 (13), 136 (6), 137 (10), 138 (15), 140 (6)

Rape, 37, 62–4, 94, 105, 120, 133 (6)
Recognition, in Aristophanes, 60; Aristotle on, 59–60, 71; function of, 61, 68–9; position of, 56; *Aspis*, 27; *Epitrepontes*, 67, 69; *Misoumenos*, 55–6; *Perikeiromene*, 23, 53–5
Returning travellers, 109–10, 139–5

Schlegel, A. W., v
Self-apostrophe, 11, 136 (6)
Shakespeare, W., 1, 10, 11, 20, 113, *The Comedy of Errors*, 12; *Timon of Athens*, 73, 86; *The Winter's Tale*, 21
Shaw, G. B., *How He Lied to Her Husband*, 24; *Mrs Warren's Profession*, 1–2
Sheridan, R. B., 1, 12, 20–1
Slave, see Stock characters
Soldier, see Stock characters
Soliloquy, 113
Sophocles, 144 (18); *Ajax*, 33; *Antigone*, 7; *Electra*, 33; *Oedipus Tyrannus*, 17, 60, 69; *Trachiniae*, 59
Souriau, É., 127 (7), 131 (4)
Spectacle, 27, 33, 118
Stage setting, 4, 14, 110, 129 (10), 142 (2)
Stock characters, 2, 4, 13, 45, 110–11, 140 (11); cook, 2, 13, 22, 35–6, 65, 81, 82, 83–4, 95, 99–102, 110–11; doctor, 32, 128 (5); foreigner, 35–6, 140 (6); misanthrope, 72–3, 89–90, 137 (13); miser (Smikrines), 13, 33, 34, 62,

Stock characters – *cont.*
64, 111, 113; old woman, 77, 83, 97, 140 (8); parasite, 13, 15, 75, 82; slave, 3, (clever) 38–40, (complaining) 47, 81, 105, (running) 75, 135 (5); soldier, 45–6, 49, 50, 111, 142 (4)

Surrogates, for principal characters, 21, 63 ,64, 74, 81, 87, 99

Terracottas, 140 (8)
Terence, 1, 12, 19, 61, 110; double plots in, 57; *Adelphoe*, 9, 25, 72, 143 (12); *Andria*, 1–2, 25, 40, 110, 114–16, 118; *Eunuchus*, 48, 49, 111, 137 (12), 142 (4); *Hecyra*, 68
Theatre building, 6, 114
Theocritus, 132 (10)
Theophrastos, 4, 6, 120
Thracians, in comedy, 36, 128 (8)
Three-Actor Rule, 131, (5), 142 (8)

Tragedy, techniques of, 17–19, 23, 61, 112–13; echoes of, 18, 33, 137 (9); parody of, 16–17, 54; plot in, 130 (1)
Turner, E. G., 50, 125 (7), 126 (8), 128 (5), 137 (9), 142 (3)

Urbanity, and soldiers, 45; theme (in *Dyskolos*) 78–9, 88, 90, 137 (11), (in *Samia*) 93, 101, 107

Whitman, C., 24, 31
Wild Oats, 19–20
Wilde, O., 12; *The Importance of Being Earnest*, 59, 61, 68, 71, 112; *Lady Windermere's Fan*, 112
Wilder, T., 4, 12
Wright, J., 109, 134 (8), 141 (1), 142 (4)

Xenarchos, 4
Xenophon, 125 (4), 143 (11)